ALI PACHA

(From Celebrated Crimes)

ALI PACHA
(From Celebrated Crimes)

ALEXANDRE DUMAS, PERE

ARC
MANOR
Rockville, MARYLAND
2008

ISBN: 978-1-60450-104-9

Published by Arc Manor
P. O. Box 10339
Rockville, md 20849-0339
www.ArcManor.com
Printed in the United States of America/United Kingdom

I

The beginning of the nineteenth century was a time of audacious enterprises and strange vicissitudes of fortune. Whilst Western Europe in turn submitted and struggled against a sub-lieutenant who made himself an emperor, who at his pleasure made kings and destroyed kingdoms, the ancient eastern part of the Continent, like mummies which preserve but the semblance of life, was gradually tumbling to pieces, and getting parcelled out amongst bold adventurers who skirmished over its ruins. Without mentioning local revolts which produced only short-lived struggles and trifling changes of administration, such as that of Djezzar Pacha, who refused to pay tribute because he thought himself impregnable in his citadel of Saint-Jean-d'Acre, or that of Passevend-Oglou Pacha, who planted himself on the walls of Widdin as defender of the Janissaries against the institution of the regular militia decreed by Sultan Selim at Stamboul, there were wider spread rebellions which attacked the constitution of the Turkish Empire and diminished its extent; amongst them that of Czerni-Georges, which raised Servia to the position of a free state; of Mahomet Ali, who made his pachalik of Egypt into a kingdom; and finally that of the man whose history we are about to narrate, Ali Tepeleni, Pacha of Janina, whose long resistance to the suzerain power preceded and brought about the regeneration of Greece.

Ali's own will counted for nothing in this important movement. He foresaw it, but without ever seeking to aid it, and was powerless to arrest it. He was not one of those men who place their lives and services at the disposal of any cause indiscriminately; and his sole aim was to acquire and increase a power of which he was both the guiding influence, and the end and object. His nature contained the seeds of every human passion, and he devoted all his long life to their development and gratification. This explains his whole temperament; his actions were merely the natural outcome of his character confronted with circumstances. Few men have understood themselves better or been on better terms with the orbit of their existence, and as the personality of an individual is all the more striking, in proportion as it reflects the manners and ideas of the time and country in which he has lived, so the figure of Ali Pacha stands out, if not one of the most brilliant, at least one of the most singular in contemporary history.

From the middle of the eighteenth century Turkey had been a prey to the political gangrene of which she is vainly trying to cure herself to-day, and which, before long, will dismember her in the sight of all Europe. Anarchy and disorder reigned from one end of the empire to the other. The Osmanli race, bred on conquest alone, proved good for nothing when conquest failed. It naturally therefore came to pass when Sobieski, who saved Christianity under the walls of Vienna, as before his time Charles Martel had saved it on the plains of Poitiers, had set bounds to the wave of Mussulman westward invasion, and definitely fixed a limit which it should not pass, that the Osmanli warlike instincts recoiled upon themselves. The haughty descendants of Ortogrul, who considered themselves born to command, seeing victory forsake them, fell back upon tyranny. Vainly did reason expostulate that oppression could not long be exercised by hands which had lost their strength, and that peace imposed new and different labours on those who no longer triumphed in war; they would listen to nothing; and, as fatalistic when condemned to a state of peace as when they marched forth conquering and to conquer, they cowered down in magnificent listlessness, leaving the whole burden of their support on conquered peoples. Like ignorant farmers, who exhaust fertile fields by forcing crops; they rapidly ruined their vast and rich empire by exorbitant exactions. Inexorable conquerors and insatiable masters, with one hand they flogged their slaves and with the other plundered them. Nothing was superior to their insolence, nothing on a level with their greed. They were never glutted, and never relaxed their extortions. But in proportion as their needs increased on the one hand, so did their resources diminish on the other. Their oppressed subjects soon found that they must escape at any cost from oppressors whom they could neither appease nor satisfy. Each population took the steps best suited to its position and character; some chose inertia, others violence. The inhabitants of the plains, powerless and shelterless, bent like reeds before the storm and evaded the shock against which they were unable to stand. The mountaineers planted themselves like rocks in a torrent, and dammed its course with all their might. On both sides arose a determined resistance, different in method, similar in result. In the case of the peasants labour came to a stand-still; in that of the hill folk open war broke out. The grasping exactions of the tyrant dominant body produced nothing from waste lands and armed mountaineers; destitution and revolt were equally beyond their power to cope with; and all that was left for tyranny to govern was a desert enclosed by a wall.

But, all the same, the wants of a magnificent sultan, descendant of the Prophet and distributor of crowns, must be supplied; and to do this, the Sublime Porte needed money. Unconsciously imitating the Roman Senate, the Turkish Divan put up the empire for sale by public auction. All employments were sold to the highest bidder; pachas, beys, cadis, ministers of every rank, and clerks of every class had to buy their posts from their sovereign and get the money back out of his subjects. They spent their money in the capital, and recuperated themselves in the provinces. And as there was no other law than their master's pleasure, so there was no other guarantee than his caprice. They had therefore to set quickly to work; the post might be lost before its cost had been recovered. Thus all the science of administration resolved itself into plundering as much and as quickly as possible. To this end, the delegate of imperial power delegated in his turn, on similar conditions, other agents to seize for him and for themselves all they could lay their hands on; so that the inhabitants of the empire might be divided into three classes – those who were striving to seize everything; those who were trying to save a little; and those who, having nothing and hoping for nothing, took no interest in affairs at all.

Albania was one of the most difficult provinces to manage. Its inhabitants were poor and brave, and the nature of the country was mountainous and inaccessible. The pachas had great difficulty in collecting tribute, because the people were given to fighting for their bread. Whether Mahomedans or Christians, the Albanians were above all soldiers. Descended on the one side from the unconquerable Scythians, on the other from the ancient Macedonians, not long since masters of the world, crossed with Norman adventurers brought eastwards by the great movement of the Crusades; they felt the blood of warriors flow in their veins, and that war was their element. Sometimes at feud with one another, canton against canton, village against village, often even house against house; sometimes rebelling against the government their sanjaks; sometimes in league with these against the sultan; they never rested from combat except in an armed peace. Each tribe had its military organisation, each family its fortified stronghold, each man his gun on his shoulder. When they had nothing better to do, they tilled their fields, or mowed their neighbours', carrying off, it should be noted, the crop; or pastured their flocks, watching the opportunity to trespass over pasture limits. This was the normal and regular life of the population of Epirus, Thesprotia, Thessaly, and Upper Albania. Lower Albania, less strong, was also less active and bold; and there, as in many other parts of Turkey, the dalesman was often the prey of the mountaineer. It was in the mountain districts where were preserved the recollections of Scander Beg, and where the manners of ancient Laconia prevailed, the deeds of the brave soldier were sung on the lyre, and the skilful robber quoted as an example to the children by the father of the family. Village feasts were held on the booty taken from strangers; and the favourite dish was always a stolen sheep. Every man was esteemed in proportion to his skill and courage, and a man's chances of making a good match were greatly enhanced when he acquired the reputation of being an agile mountaineer and a good bandit.

The Albanians proudly called this anarchy liberty, and religiously guarded a state of disorder bequeathed by their ancestors, which always assured the first place to the most valiant.

It was amidst men and manners such as these that Ali Tepeleni was born. He boasted that he belonged to the conquering race, and that he descended from an ancient Anatolian family which had crossed into Albania with the troops of Bajazet Ilderim. But it is made certain by the learned researches of M. de Pouqueville that he sprang from a native stock, and not an Asiatic one, as he pretended. His ancestors were Christian Skipetars, who became Mussulmans after the Turkish invasion, and his ancestry certainly cannot be traced farther back than the end of the sixteenth century.

Mouktar Tepeleni, his grandfather, perished in the Turkish expedition against Corfu, in 1716. Marshal Schullemburg, who defended the island, having repulsed the enemy with loss, took Mouktar prisoner on Mount San Salvador, where he was in charge of a signalling party, and with a barbarity worthy of his adversaries, hung him without trial. It must be admitted that the memory of this murder must have had the effect of rendering Ali badly disposed towards Christians.

Mouktar left three sons, two of whom, Salik and Mahomet, were born of the same mother, a lawful wife, but the mother of the youngest, Veli, was a slave. His origin was no legal bar to his succeeding like his brothers. The family was one of the richest in the town of Tepelen, whose name it bore; it enjoyed an income of six thousand piastres, equal to twenty thousand francs. This was a large fortune in a poor country, where, all commodities were cheap. But the Tepeleni family, holding the rank of beys, had to maintain a state like that of the great financiers of feudal Europe. They had to keep a large stud of horses, with a great retinue of servants and men-at-arms, and consequently to incur heavy expenses; thus they constantly found their revenue inadequate. The most natural means of raising it which occurred to them was to diminish the number of those who shared it; therefore the two elder brothers, sons of the wife, combined against Veli, the son of the slave, and drove him out of the house. The latter, forced to leave home, bore his fate like a brave man, and determined to levy exactions on others to compensate him for the losses incurred through his brothers. He became a freebooter, patrolling highroads and lanes, with his gun on his shoulder and his yataghan in his belt, attacking, holding for ransom, or plundering all whom he encountered.

After some years of this profitable business, he found himself a wealthy man and chief of a warlike band. Judging that the moment for vengeance had arrived, he marched for Tepelen, which he reached unsuspected, crossed the river Vojutza, the ancient Aous, penetrated the streets unresisted, and presented himself before the paternal house, in which his brothers, forewarned, had barricaded themselves. He at once besieged them, soon forced the gates, and pursued them to a tent, in which they took a final refuge. He surrounded this tent, waited till they were inside it, and then set fire to the four corners. "See," said he to those around him, "they cannot accuse me of vindictive reprisals; my brothers drove me out of doors, and I retaliate by keeping them at home for ever."

In a few moments he was his father's sole heir and master of Tepelen. Arrived at the summit of his ambition, he gave up free-booting, and established himself in the town, of which he became chief ago. He had already a son by a slave, who soon presented him with another son, and afterwards with a daughter, so that he had no reason to fear dying without an heir. But finding himself rich enough to maintain more wives and bring up many children, he desired to increase his credit by allying himself to some great family of the country. He therefore solicited and obtained the hand of Kamco, daughter of a bey of Conitza. This marriage attached him by the ties of relationship to the principal families of the province, among others to Kourd Pacha, Vizier of Serat, who was descended from the illustrious race of Scander Beg. After a few years, Veli had by his new wife a son named Ali, the subject of this history, and a daughter named Chainitza.

In spite of his intentions to reform, Veli could not entirely give up his old habits. Although his fortune placed him altogether above small gains and losses, he continued to amuse himself by raiding from time to time sheep, goats, and other perquisites, probably to keep his hand in. This innocent exercise of his taste was not to the fancy of his neighbours, and brawls and fights recommenced in fine style. Fortune did not always favour him, and the old mountaineer lost in the town part of what he had made on the hills. Vexations soured his temper and injured his health. Notwithstanding the injunctions of Mahomet, he sought consolation in wine, which soon closed his career. He died in 1754.

II

Ali thus at thirteen years of age was free to indulge in the impetuosity of his character. From his early youth he had manifested a mettle and activity rare in young Turks, haughty by nature and self-restrained by education. Scarcely out of the nursery, he spent his time in climbing mountains, wandering through forests, scaling precipices, rolling in snow, inhaling the wind, defying the tempests, breathing out his nervous energy through every pore. Possibly he learnt in the midst of every kind of danger to brave everything and subdue everything; possibly in sympathy with the majesty of nature, he felt aroused in him a need of personal grandeur which nothing could satiate. In vain his father sought to calm his savage temper, and restrain his vagabond spirit; nothing was of any use. As obstinate as intractable, he set at defiance all efforts and all precautions. If they shut him up, he broke the door or jumped out of the window; if they threatened him, he pretended to comply, conquered by fear, and promised everything that was required, but only to break his word the first opportunity. He had a tutor specially attached to his person and charged to supervise all his actions. He constantly deluded him by fresh tricks, and when he thought himself free from the consequences, he maltreated him with gross violence. It was only in his youth, after his father's death, that he became more manageable; he even consented to learn to read, to please his mother, whose idol he was, and to whom in return he gave all his affection.

If Kamco had so strong a liking for Ali, it was because she found in him, not only her blood, but also her character. During the lifetime of her husband, whom she feared, she seemed only an ordinary woman; but as soon as his eyes were closed, she gave free scope to the violent passions which agitated her bosom. Ambitious, bold, vindictive, she assiduously culti-vated the germs of ambition, hardihood, and vengeance which already strongly showed themselves in the young Ali. "My son," she was never tired of telling him, "he who cannot defend his patrimony richly deserves to lose it. Remember that the property of others is only theirs so long as they are strong enough to keep it, and that when you find yourself strong enough to take it from them, it is yours. Success justifies everything, and everything is permissible to him who has the power to do it."

Ali, when he reached the zenith of his greatness, used to declare that his success was entirely his mother's work. "I owe everything to my mother," he said one day to the French Consul; "for my father, when he died, left me nothing but a den of wild beasts and a few fields. My imagination, inflamed by the counsels of her who has given me life twice over, since she has made me both a man and a vizier, revealed to me the secret of my destiny. Thenceforward I saw nothing in Tepelen but the natal air from which I was to spring on the prey which I devoured mentally. I dreamt of nothing else but power, treasures, palaces, in short what time has realised and still promises; for the point I have now reached is not the limit of my hopes."

Kamco did not confine herself to words; she employed every means to increase the fortune of her beloved son and to make him a power. Her first care was to poison the children of Veli's favourite slave, who had died before him. Then, at ease about the interior of her family, she di-rected her attention to the exterior. Renouncing all the habit of her sex, she abandoned the veil and the distaff, and took up arms, under pre-text of maintaining the rights of her children. She collected round her her husband's old partisans, whom she attached to her service, some by presents, others by various favours, and she gradually enlisted all the lawless and adventurous men in Toscaria. With their aid, she made herself all powerful in Tepelen, and inflicted the most rigorous persecu-tions on such as remained hostile to her.

But the inhabitants of the two adjacent villages of Kormovo and Kar-diki, fearing lest this terrible woman, aided by her son, now grown into a man, should strike a blow against their independence, made a secret alliance against her, with the object of putting her out of the way the first convenient opportunity. Learning one day that Ali had started on a distant expedition with his best soldiers; they surprised Tepelen under cover of night, and carried off Kamco and her daughter Chainitza captives to Kardiki. It was proposed to put them to death; and sufficient evidence to justify their execution was not wanting, but their beauty saved their lives; their captors preferred to revenge themselves by licentiousness rather than by murder. Shut up all day in prison, they only emerged at night to pass into the arms of the men who had won them by lot the previous morning. This state of things lasted for a month, at the end of which a Greek of Argyro-Castron, named G. Malicovo, moved by compassion for their horrible fate, ransomed them for twenty thousand piastres, and took them back to Tepelen.

Ali had just returned. He was accosted by his mother and sister, pale with fatigue, shame, and rage. They told him what had taken place, with cries and tears, and Kamco added, fixing her distracted eyes upon him, "My son! my son! my soul will enjoy no peace till Kormovo and Kardiki destroyed by thy scimitar, will no longer exist to bear witness to my dishonour."

Ali, in whom this sight and this story had aroused sanguinary passions, promised a vengeance proportioned to the outrage, and worked with all his might to place himself in a position to keep his word. A worthy son of his father, he had commenced life in the fashion of the heroes of ancient Greece, stealing sheep and goats, and from the age of fourteen years he had acquired an equal reputation to that earned by the son of Jupiter and Maia. When he grew to manhood, he extended his operations. At the time of which we are speaking, he had long practised open pillage. His plundering expeditions added to his mother's savings, who since her return from Kardiki had altogether withdrawn from public life, and devoted herself to household duties, enabled him to collect a considerable force for am expedition against Kormovo, one of the two towns he had sworn to destroy. He marched against it at the head of his banditti, but found himself vigorously opposed, lost part of his force, and was obliged to save himself and the rest by flight. He did not stop till he reached Tepelen, where he had a warm reception from Kamco, whose thirst for vengeance had been disappointed by his defeat. "Go!" said she, "go, coward! go spin with the women in the harem! The distaff is a better weapon for you than the scimitar!" The young man answered not a word, but, deeply wounded by these reproaches, retired to hide his humiliation in the bosom of his old friend the mountain. The popular legend, always thirsting for the marvelous in the adventures of heroes, has it that he found in the ruins of a church a treasure which enabled him to reconstitute his party. But he himself has contradicted this story, stating that it was by the ordinary methods of rapine and plunder that he replenished his finances. He selected from his old band of brigands thirty palikars, and entered, as their bouloubachi, or leader of the group, into the service of the Pacha of Negropont. But he soon tired of the methodical life he was obliged to lead, and passed into Thessaly, where, following the example of his father Veli, he employed his time in brigandage on the highways. Thence he raided the Pindus chain of mountains, plundered a great number of villages, and returned to Tepelen, richer and consequently more esteemed than ever.

He employed his fortune and influence in collecting a formidable guerilla force, and resumed his plundering operations. Kurd Pacha soon found himself compelled, by the universal outcry of the province, to take active measures against this young brigand. He sent against him a division of troops, which defeated him and brought him prisoner with his men to Berat, the capital of Central Albania and residence of the governor. The country flattered itself that at length it was freed from its scourge. The whole body of bandits was condemned to death; but Ali was not the man to surrender his life so easily. Whilst they were hanging his comrades, he threw himself at the feet of the pacha and begged for mercy in the name of his parents, excusing himself on account of his youth, and promising a lasting reform. The pacha, seeing at his feet a comely youth, with fair hair and blue eyes, a persuasive voice, and eloquent tongue, and in whose veins flowed the same blood as his own, was moved with pity and pardoned him. Ali got off with a mild captivity in the palace of his powerful relative, who heaped benefits upon him, and did all he could to lead him into the paths of probity. He appeared amenable to these good influences, and bitterly to repent his past errors. After some years, believing in his reformation, and moved by the prayers of Kamco, who incessantly implored the restitution of her dear son, the generous pacha restored him his liberty, only giving him to understand that he had no more mercy to expect if he again disturbed the public peace. Ali taking the threat seriously did not run the risk of braving it, and, on the contrary, did all he could to conciliate the man whose anger he dared not kindle. Not only did he keep the promise he had made to live quietly, but by his good conduct he caused his former escapades to be forgotten, putting under obligation all his neighbours, and attaching to himself, through the services he rendered them, a great number of friendly disposed persons. In this manner he soon assumed a distinguished and honourable rank among the beys of the country, and being of marriageable age, he sought and formed an alliance with the daughter of Capelan Tigre, Pacha of Delvino, who resided at Argyro-Castron. This union, happy on both sides, gave him, with one of the most accomplished women in Epirus, a high position and great influence.

It seemed as if this marriage were destined to wean Ali forever from his former turbulent habits and wild adventures. But the family into which he had married afforded violent contrasts and equal elements of good and mischief. If Emineh, his wife, was a model of virtue, his father-in-law, Capelan, was a composition of every vice – selfish, ambitious, turbulent, fierce. Confident in his courage, and further emboldened by his remoteness from the capital, the Pacha of Delvino gloried in setting law and authority at defiance.

Ali's disposition was too much like that of his father-in-law to prevent him from taking his measure very quickly. He soon got on good terms with him, and entered into his schemes, waiting for an opportunity to denounce him and become his successor. For this opportunity he had not long to wait.

Capelan's object in giving his daughter to Tepeleni was to enlist him among the beys of the province to gain independence, the ruling passion of viziers. The cunning young man pretended to enter into the views of his father-in-law, and did all he could to urge him into the path of rebellion.

An adventurer named Stephano Piccolo, an emissary of Russia, had just raised in Albania the standard of the Cross and called to arms all the Christians of the Acroceraunian Mountains. The Divan sent orders to all the pachas of Northern Turkey in Europe to instantly march against the insurgents and quell the rising in blood.

Instead of obeying the orders of the Divan and joining Kurd Pacha, who had summoned him, Capelan, at the instigation of his son-in-law, did all he could to embarrass the movement of the imperial troops, and without openly making common cause with the insurgents, he rendered them substantial aid in their resistance. They were, notwithstanding, conquered and dispersed; and their chief, Stephano Piccolo, had to take refuge in the unexplored caves of Montenegro.

When the struggle was over, Capelan, as Ali had foreseen, was summoned to give an account of his conduct before the roumeli-valicy, supreme judge over Turkey in Europe. He was not only accused of the gravest offences, but proofs of them were forwarded to the Divan by the very man who had instigated them. There could be no doubt as to the result of the inquiry; therefore, the pacha, who had no suspicions of his son-in-law's duplicity, determined not to leave his pachalik. That was not in accordance with the plans of Ali, who wished to succeed to both the government and the wealth of his father-in-law. He accordingly made the most plausible remonstrances against the inefficacy and danger of such a resistance. To refuse to plead was tantamount to a confession of guilt, and was certain to bring on his head a storm against which he was powerless to cope, whilst if he obeyed the orders of the roumeli-valicy he would find it easy to excuse himself. To give more effect to his perfidious advice, Ali further employed the innocent Emineh, who was easily alarmed on her father's account. Overcome by the reasoning of his son-in-law and the tears of his daughter, the unfortunate pacha consented to go to Monastir, where he had been summoned to appear, and where he was immediately arrested and beheaded.

Ali's schemes had succeeded, but both his ambition and his cupidity were frustrated. Ali, Bey of Argyro-Castron, who had throughout shown himself devoted to the sultan, was nominated Pacha of Delvino in place of Capelan. He sequestered all the property of his predecessor, as confiscated to the sultan, and thus deprived Ali Tepeleni of all the fruits of his crime.

This disappointment kindled the wrath of the ambitious Ali. He swore vengeance for the spoliation of which he considered himself the victim. But the moment was not favourable for putting his projects in train. The murder of Capelan, which its perpetrator intended for a mere crime, proved a huge blunder. The numerous enemies of Tepeleni, silent under the administration of the late pacha, whose resentment they had cause to fear, soon made common cause under the new one, for whose support they had hopes. Ali saw the danger, sought and found the means to obviate it. He succeeded in making a match between Ali of Argyro-Castron, who was unmarried, and Chainitza, his own sister. This alliance secured to him the government of Tigre, which he held under Capelan. But that was not sufficient. He must put himself in a state of security against the dangers he had lately experienced, and establish himself on a firm footing against possible accidents. He soon formed a plan, which he himself described to the French Consul in the following words: –

"Years were elapsing," said he, "and brought no important change in my position. I was an important partisan, it is true, and strongly supported, but I held no title or Government employment of my own. I recognised the necessity of establishing myself firmly in my birthplace. I had devoted friends, and formidable foes bent on my destruction whom I must put out of the way for my own safety. I set about a plan for destroying them at one blow, and ended by devising one with which I ought to have commenced my career. Had I done so, I should have saved much time and pains.

"I was in the habit of going every day, after hunting, for a siesta in a neighbouring wood. A confidential servant of mine suggested to my enemies the idea of surprising me and assassinating me there. I myself supplied the plan of the conspiracy, which was adopted. On the day agreed upon, I preceded my adversaries to the place where I was accustomed to repose, and caused a goat to be pinioned and muzzled, and fastened under the tree, covered with my cape; I then returned home by a roundabout path. Soon after I had left, the conspirators arrived, and fired a volley at the goat.

"They ran up to make certain of my death, but were interrupted by a piquet of my men, who unexpectedly emerged from a copse where I had posted them, and they were obliged to return to Tepelen, which they entered, riotous with joy, crying 'Ali Bey is dead, now we are free!' This news reached my harem, and I heard the cries of my mother and my wife mingled with the shouts of my enemies. I allowed the commotion to run its course and reach its height, so as to indicate which were my friends and which my foes. But when the former were at the depth of their distress and the latter at the height of their joy, and, exulting in their supposed victory, had drowned their prudence and their courage in floods of wine, then, strong in the justice of my cause, I appeared upon the scene. Now was the time for my friends to triumph and for my foes to tremble. I set to work at the head of my partisans, and before sunrise had exterminated the last of my enemies. I distributed their lands, their houses, and their goods amongst my followers, and from that moment I could call the town of Tepelen my own."

A less ambitious man might perhaps have remained satisfied with such a result. But Ali did not look upon the suzerainty of a canton as a final object, but only as a means to an end; and he had not made himself master of Tepelen to limit himself to a petty state, but to employ it as a base of operations.

He had allied himself to Ali of Argyro-Castron to get rid of his enemies; once free from them, he began to plot against his supplanter.

He forgot neither his vindictive projects nor his ambitious schemes. As prudent in execution as bold in design, he took good care not to openly attack a man stronger than himself, and gained by stratagem what he could not obtain by violence. The honest and straightforward character of his brother-in-law afforded an easy success to his perfidy. He began by endeavouring to suborn his sister Chainitza, and several times proposed to her to poison her husband; but she, who dearly loved the pacha, who was a kind husband and to whom she had borne two children, repulsed his suggestions with horror, and threatened, if he persisted, to denounce him. Ali, fearing the consequences if she carried out her threat, begged forgiveness for his wicked plans, pretended deep repentance, and spoke of his brother-in-law in terms of the warmest affection. His acting was so consummate that even Chainitza, who well knew her brother's subtle character, was deceived by it. When he saw that she was his dupe, knowing that he had nothing more either to fear or to hope for from that side, he directed his attention to another.

The pacha had a brother named Soliman, whose character nearly resembled that of Tepeleni. The latter, after having for some time quietly studied him, thought he discerned in him the man he wanted; he tempted him to kill the pacha, offering him, as the price of this crime, his whole inheritance and the hand of Chainitza, only reserving for himself the long coveted sanjak. Soliman accepted the proposals, and the fratricidal bargain was concluded. The two conspirators, sole masters of the secret, the horrible nature of which guaranteed their mutual fidelity, and having free access to the person of their victim, could not fail in their object.

One day, when they were both received by the pacha in private audience, Soliman, taking advantage of a moment when he was unobserved, drew a pistol from his belt and blew out his brother's brains. Chainitza ran at the sound, and saw her husband lying dead between her brother and her brother-in-law. Her cries for help were stopped by threats of death if she moved or uttered a sound. As she lay, fainting with grief and terror, Ali made a sign to Soliman, who covered her with his cloak, and declared her his wife. Ali pronounced the marriage concluded, and retired for it to be consummated. Thus was celebrated this frightful wedding, in the scene of an awful crime, beside the corpse of a man who a moment before had been the husband of the bride and the brother of the bridegroom.

The assassins published the death of the pacha, attributing it, as is usual in Turkey, to a fit of cerebral apoplexy. But the truth soon leaked out from the lying shrouds in which it had been wrapped. Reports even exceeded the truth, and public opinion implicated Chainitza in a crime of which she had been but the witness. Appearances certainly justified these suspicions. The young wife had soon consoled herself in the arms of her second husband for the loss of the first, and her son by him presently died suddenly, thus leaving Soliman in lawful and peaceful possession of all his brother's wealth. As for the little girl, as she had no rights and could hurt no one, her life was spared and she was eventually married to a bey of Cleisoura, destined in the sequel to cut a tragic figure in the history of the Tepeleni family.

But Ali was once more deprived of the fruit of his bloody schemes. Notwithstanding all his intrigues, the sanjak of Delvino was conferred, not upon him, but upon a bey of one of the first families of Zapouria. But, far from being discouraged, he recommenced with new boldness and still greater confidence the work of his elevation, so often begun and so often interrupted. He took advantage of his increasing influence to ingratiate himself with the new pacha, and was so successful in insinuating himself into his confidence, that he was received into the palace and treated like the pacha's son. There he acquired complete knowledge of the details of the pachalik and the affairs of the pacha, preparing himself to govern the one when he had got rid of the other.

The sanjak of Delvino was bounded from Venetian territory by the district of Buthrotum. Selim, a better neighbour and an abler politician than his predecessors, sought to renew and preserve friendly commercial relations with the purveyors of the Magnificent Republic. This wise conduct, equally advantageous for both the bordering provinces, instead of gaining for the pacha the praise and favours which he deserved, rendered him suspected at a court whose sole political idea was hatred of the name of Christian, and whose sole means of government was terror. Ali immediately perceived the pacha's error, and the advantage which he himself could derive from it. Selim, as one of his commercial transactions with the Venetians, had sold them, for a number of years, the right of felling timber in a forest near Lake Reloda. Ali immediately took advantage of this to denounce the pacha as guilty of having alienated the territory of the Sublime Porte, and of a desire to deliver to the infidels all the province of Delvino. Masking his ambitious designs under the veil of religion and patriotism, he lamented, in his denunciatory report, the necessity under which he found himself, as a loyal subject and faithful

Mussulman, of accusing a man who had been his benefactor, and thus at the same time gained the benefit of crime and the credit of virtue.

Under the gloomy despotism of the Turks, a man in any position of responsibility is condemned almost as soon as accused; and if he is not strong enough to inspire terror, his ruin is certain. Ali received at Tepelen, where he had retired to more conveniently weave his perfidious plots, an order to get rid of the pacha. At the receipt of the firman of execution he leaped with joy, and flew to Delvino to seize the prey which was abandoned to him.

The noble Selim, little suspecting that his protege had become his accuser and was preparing to become his executioner, received him with more tenderness than ever, and lodged him, as heretofore, in his palace. Under the shadow of this hospitable roof, Ali skilfully prepared the consummation of the crime which was for ever to draw him out of obscurity. He went every morning to pay his court to the pacha, whose confidence he doubted; then, one day, feigning illness, he sent excuses for inability to pay his respects to a man whom he was accustomed to regard as his father, and begged him to come for a moment into his apartment. The invitation being accepted, he concealed assassins in one of the cupboards without shelves, so common in the East, which contain by day the mattresses spread by night on the floor for the slaves to sleep upon. At the hour fixed, the old man arrived. Ali rose from his sofa with a depressed air, met him, kissed the hem of his robe, and, after seating him in his place, himself offered him a pipe-and-coffee, which were accepted. But instead of putting the cup in the hand stretched to receive it, he let it fall on the floor, where it broke into a thousand pieces. This was the signal. The assassins sprang from their retreat and darted upon Selim, who fell, exclaiming, like Caesar, "And it is thou, my son, who takest my life!"

At the sound of the tumult which followed the assassination, Selim's bodyguard, running up, found Ali erect, covered with blood, surrounded by assassins, holding in his hand the firman displayed, and crying with a menacing voice, "I have killed the traitor Selim by the order of our glorious sultan; here is his imperial command." At these words, and the sight of the fatal diploma, all prostrated themselves terror-stricken. Ali, after ordering the decapitation of Selim, whose head he seized as a trophy, ordered the cadi, the beys, and the Greek archons to meet at the palace to prepare the official account of the execution of the sentence. They assembled, trembling; the sacred hymn of the Fatahat was sung, and the murder declared legal, in the name of the merciful and compassionate God, Lord of the world.

When they had sealed up the effects of the victim, the murderer left the palace, taking with him, as a hostage, Mustapha, son of Selim, destined to be even more unfortunate than his father.

A few days afterwards, the Divan awarded to Ali Tepeleni, as a reward for his zeal for the State and religion, the sanjak of Thessaly, with the title of Dervendgi-pacha, or Provost Marshal of the roads. This latter dignity was conferred on the condition of his levying a body of four thousand men to clear the valley of the Peneus of a multitude of Christian chiefs who exercised more power than the officers of the Grand Seigneur. The new pacha took advantage of this to enlist a numerous body of Albanians ready for any enterprise, and completely devoted to him. With two important commands, and with this strong force at his back, he repaired to Trikala, the seat of his government, where he speedily acquired great influence.

His first act of authority was to exterminate the bands of Armatolis, or Christian militia, which infested the plain. He laid violent hands on all whom he caught, and drove the rest back into their mountains, splitting them up into small bands whom he could deal with at his pleasure. At the same time he sent a few heads to Constantinople, to amuse the sultan and the mob, and some money to the ministers to gain their support. "For," said he, "water sleeps, but envy never does." These steps were prudent, and whilst his credit increased at court, order was reestablished from the defiles of the Perrebia of Pindus to the vale of Tempe and to the pass of Thermopylae.

These exploits of the provost-marshal, amplified by Oriental exaggeration, justified the ideas which were entertained of the capacity of Ali Pacha. Impatient of celebrity, he took good care himself to spread his fame, relating his prowess to all comers, making presents to the sultan's officers who came into his government, and showing travellers his palace courtyard festooned with decapitated heads. But what chiefly tended to consolidate his power was the treasure which he ceaselessly amassed by every means. He never struck for the mere pleasure of striking, and the numerous victims of his proscriptions only perished to enrich him. His death sentences always fell on beys and wealthy persons whom he wished to plunder. In his eyes the axe was but an instrument of fortune, and the executioner a tax-gatherer.

III

Having governed Thessaly in this manner during several years, Ali found himself in a position to acquire the province of Janina, the possession of which, by making him master of Epirus, would enable him to crush all his enemies and to reign supreme over the three divisions of Albania.

But before he could succeed in this, it was necessary to dispose of the pacha already in possession. Fortunately for Ali, the latter was a weak and indolent man, quite incapable of struggling against so formidable a rival; and his enemy speedily conceived and put into execution a plan intended to bring about the fulfilment of his desires. He came to terms with the same Armatolians whom he had formerly treated so harshly, and let them loose, provided with arms and ammunition, on the country which he wished to obtain. Soon the whole region echoed with stories of devastation and pillage. The pacha, unable to repel the incursions of these mountaineers, employed the few troops he had in oppressing the inhabitants of the plains, who, groaning under both extortion and rapine, vainly filled the air with their despairing cries. Ali hoped that the Divan, which usually judged only after the event, seeing that Epirus lay desolate, while Thessaly flourished under his own administration, would, before long, entrust himself with the government of both provinces, when a family incident occurred, which for a time diverted the course of his political manoeuvres.

For a long time his mother Kamco had suffered from an internal cancer, the result of a life of depravity. Feeling that her end drew near, she despatched messenger after messenger, summoning her son to her bedside.

He started, but arrived too late, and found only his sister Chainitza mourning over the body of their mother, who had expired in her arms an hour previously. Breathing unutterable rage and pronouncing horrible imprecations against Heaven, Kamco had commanded her children, under pain of her dying curse, to carry out her last wishes faithfully. After having long given way to their grief, Ali and Chainitza read together the document which contained these commands. It ordained some special assassinations, mentioned sundry villages which, some day, were to be given to the flames, but ordered them most especially, as soon as possible, to exterminate the inhabitants of Kormovo and Kardiki, from whom she had endured the last horrors of slavery.

Then, after advising her children to remain united, to enrich their soldiers, and to count as nothing people who were useless to them, Kamco ended by commanding them to send in her name a pilgrim to Mecca, who should deposit an offering on the tomb of the Prophet for the repose of her soul. Having perused these last injunctions, Ali and Chainitza joined hands, and over the inanimate remains of their departed mother swore to accomplish her dying behests.

The pilgrimage came first under consideration. Now a pilgrim can only be sent as proxy to Mecca, or offerings be made at the tomb of Medina, at the expense of legitimately acquired property duly sold for the purpose. The brother and sister made a careful examination of the family estates, and after long hunting, thought they had found the correct thing in a small property of about fifteen hundred francs income, inherited from their great-grandfather, founder of the Tepel-Enian dynasty. But further investigations disclosed that even this last resource had been forcibly taken from a Christian, and the idea of a pious pilgrimage and a sacred offering had to be given up. They then agreed to atone for the impossibility of expiation by the grandeur of their vengeance, and swore to pursue without ceasing and to destroy without mercy all enemies of their family.

The best mode of carrying out this terrible and self-given pledge was that Ali should resume his plans of aggrandizement exactly where he had left them. He succeeded in acquiring the pachalik of Janina, which was granted him by the Porte under the title of "arpalik," or conquest. It was an old custom, natural to the warlike habits of the Turks, to bestow the Government provinces or towns affecting to despise the authority of the Grand Seigneur or whomsoever succeeded in controlling them, and

Janina occupied this position. It was principally inhabited by Albanians, who had an enthusiastic admiration for anarchy, dignified by them with the name of "Liberty," and who thought themselves independent in proportion to the disturbance they succeeded in making. Each lived retired as if in a mountain castle, and only went out in order to participate in the quarrels of his faction in the forum. As for the pachas, they were relegated to the old castle on the lake, and there was no difficulty in obtaining their recall.

Consequently there was a general outcry at the news of Ali Pacha's nomination, and it was unanimously agreed that a man whose character and power were alike dreaded must not be admitted within the walls of Janina. Ali, not choosing to risk his forces in an open battle with a warlike population, and preferring a slower and safer way to a short and dangerous one, began by pillaging the villages and farms belonging to his most powerful opponents. His tactics succeeded, and the very persons who had been foremost in vowing hatred to the son of Kamco and who had sworn most loudly that they would die rather than submit to the tyrant, seeing their property daily ravaged, and impending ruin if hostilities continued, applied themselves to procure peace. Messengers were sent secretly to Ali, offering to admit him into Janina if he would undertake to respect the lives and property of his new allies. Ali promised whatever they asked, and entered the town by night. His first proceeding was to appear before the cadi, whom he compelled to register and proclaim his firmans of investiture.

In the same year in which he arrived at this dignity, really the desire and object of Ali's whole life, occurred also the death of the Sultan Abdul Hamid, whose two sons, Mustapha and Mahmoud, were confined in the Old Seraglio. This change of rulers, however, made no difference to Ali; the peaceful Selim, exchanging the prison to which his nephews were now relegated, for the throne of their father, confirmed the Pacha of Janina in the titles, offices, and privileges which had been conferred on him.

Established in his position by this double investiture, Ali applied himself to the definite settlement of his claims. He was now fifty years of age, and was at the height of his intellectual development: experience had been his teacher, and the lesson of no single event had been lost upon him. An uncultivated but just and penetrating mind enabled him to comprehend facts, analyse causes, and anticipate results; and as his heart never interfered with the deductions of his rough intelligence, he had by a sort of logical sequence formulated an inflexible plan of action. This man, wholly ignorant, not only of the ideas of history but also of the great names of Europe, had succeeded in divining, and as a natural consequence of his active and practical character, in also realising Macchiavelli, as is amply shown in the expansion of his greatness and the exercise of his power. Without faith in God, despising men, loving and thinking only of himself, distrusting all around him, audacious in design, immovable in resolution, inexorable in execution, merciless in vengeance, by turns insolent, humble, violent, or supple according to circumstances, always and entirely logical in his egotism, he is Cesar Borgia reborn as a Mussulman; he is the incarnate ideal of Florentine policy, the Italian prince converted into a satrap.

Age had as yet in no way impaired Ali's strength and activity, and nothing prevented his profiting by the advantages of his position. Already possessing great riches, which every day he saw increasing under his management, he maintained a large body of warlike and devoted troops, he united the offices of Pacha of two tails of Janina, of Toparch of Thessaly, and of Provost Marshal of the Highway. As influential aids both to his reputation for general ability and the terror of his arms, and his authority as ruler, there stood by his side two sons, Mouktar and Veli, offspring of his wife Emineh, both fully grown and carefully educated in the principles of their father.

Ali's first care, once master of Janina, was to annihilate the beys forming the aristocracy of the place, whose hatred he was well aware of, and whose plots he dreaded. He ruined them all, banishing many and putting others to death. Knowing that he must make friends to supply the vacancy caused by the destruction of his foes, he enriched with the spoil the Albanian mountaineers in his pay, known by the name of Skipetars, on whom he conferred most of the vacant employments. But much too prudent to allow all the power to fall into the hands of a single caste, although a foreign one to the capital, he, by a singular innovation, added to and mixed with them an infusion of Orthodox Greeks, a skilful but despised race, whose talents he could use without having to dread their influence. While thus endeavouring on one side to destroy the power of his enemies by depriving them of both authority and wealth, and on the other to consolidate his own by establishing a firm administration, he neglected no means of acquiring popularity. A fervent disciple of Mahomet when among fanatic Mussulmans, a materialist with the Bektagis who professed a rude pantheism, a Christian among the Greeks, with whom he drank to the health of the Holy Virgin, he made everywhere partisans by flattering the idea most in vogue. But if he constantly changed both opinions and language when dealing with subordinates whom it was desirable to win over, Ali towards his superiors had one only line of conduct which he never transgressed. Obsequious towards the Sublime Porte, so long as it did not interfere with his private authority, he not only paid with exactitude all dues to the sultan, to whom he even often advanced money, but he also pensioned the most influential ministers. He was bent on having no enemies who could really injure his power, and he knew that in an absolute government no conviction can hold its own against the power of gold.

Having thus annihilated the nobles, deceived the multitude with plausible words, and lulled to sleep the watchfulness of the Divan, Ali resolved to turn his arms against Kormovo. At the foot of its rocks he had, in youth, experienced the disgrace of defeat, and during thirty nights Kamco and Chainitza had endured all horrors of outrage at the hands of its warriors. Thus the implacable pacha had a twofold wrong to punish, a double vengeance to exact.

This time, profiting by experience, he called in the aid of treachery. Arrived at the citadel, he negotiated, promised an amnesty, forgiveness for all, actual rewards for some. The inhabitants, only too happy to make peace with so formidable an adversary, demanded and obtained a truce to settle the conditions. This was exactly what Ali expected, and Kormovo, sleeping on the faith of the treaty, was suddenly attacked and taken. All who did not escape by flight perished by the sword in the darkness, or by the hand of the executioner the next morning. Those who had offered violence aforetime to Ali's mother and sister were carefully sought for, and whether convicted or merely accused, were impaled on spits, torn with redhot pincers, and slowly roasted between two fires; the women were shaved and publicly scourged, and then sold as slaves.

This vengeance, in which all the nobles of the province not yet entirely ruined were compelled to assist, was worth a decisive victory to Ali. Towns, cantons, whole districts, overwhelmed with terror, submitted without striking a blow, and his name, joined to the recital of a massacre which ranked as a glorious exploit in the eyes of this savage people, echoed like thunder from valley to valley and mountain to mountain. In order that all surrounding him might participate in the joy of his success Ali gave his army a splendid festival. Of unrivalled activity, and, Mohammedan only in name, he himself led the chorus in the Pyrrhic and Klephtic dances, the ceremonials of warriors and of robbers. There was no lack of wine, of sheep, goats, and lambs roasted before enormous fires; made of the debris of the ruined city; antique games of archery and wrestling were celebrated, and the victors received their prizes from the hand of their chief. The plunder, slaves, and cattle were then shared, and the Tapygae, considered as the lowest of the four tribes composing the race of Skipetars, and ranking as the refuse of the army, carried off into the mountains of Acroceraunia, doors, windows, nails, and even the tiles of the houses, which were then all surrendered to the flames.

However, Ibrahim, the successor and son-in-law of Kurd Pacha, could not see with indifference part of his province invaded by his ambitious neighbour. He complained and negotiated, but obtaining no satisfaction, called out an army composed of Skipetars of Toxid, all Islamites, and gave the command to his brother Sepher, Bey of Avlone. Ali, who had adopted the policy of opposing alternately the Cross to the Crescent and the Crescent to the Cross, summoned to his aid the Christian chiefs of the mountains, who descended into the plains at the head of their unconquered troops. As is generally the case in Albania, where war is merely an excuse for brigandage, instead of deciding matters by a pitched battle, both sides contented themselves with burning villages, hanging peasants, and carrying off cattle.

Also, in accordance with the custom of the country, the women interposed between the combatants, and the good and gentle Emineh laid proposals of peace before Ibrahim Pacha, to whose apathetic disposition a state of war was disagreeable, and who was only too happy to conclude a fairly satisfactory negotiation. A family alliance was arranged, in virtue of which Ali retained his conquests, which were considered as the marriage portion of Ibrahim's eldest daughter, who became the wife of Ali's eldest son, Mouktar.

It was hoped that this peace might prove permanent, but the marriage which sealed the treaty was barely concluded before a fresh quarrel broke out between the pachas. Ali, having wrung such important concessions from the weakness of his neighbour, desired to obtain yet more. But closely allied to Ibrahim were two persons gifted with great firmness of character and unusual ability, whose position gave them great influence. They were his wife Zaidee, and his brother Sepher, who had been in command during the war just terminated. As both were inimical to Ali, who could not hope to corrupt them, he latter resolved to get rid of them.

Having in the days of his youth been intimate with Kurd Pacha, Ali had endeavoured to seduce his daughter, already the wife of Ibrahim. Being discovered by the latter in the act of scaling the wall of his harem, he had been obliged to fly the country. Wishing now to ruin the woman whom he had formerly tried to corrupt, Ali sought to turn his former crime to the success of a new one. Anonymous letters, secretly sent to Ibrahim, warned him that his wife intended to poison him, in order to be able later to marry Ali Pacha, whom she had always loved. In a country like Turkey, where to suspect a woman is to accuse her, and accusation is synonymous with condemnation, such a calumny might easily cause the death of the innocent Zaidee. But if Ibrahim was weak and indolent, he was also confiding and generous. He took the letters to his wife, who had no difficulty in clearing herself, and who warned him against the writer, whose object and plots she easily divined, so that this odious conspiracy turned only to Ali's discredit. But the latter was not likely either to concern himself as to what others said or thought about him or to be disconcerted by a failure. He simply turned his machinations against his other enemy, and arranged matters this time so as to avoid a failure.

He sent to Zagori, a district noted for its doctors, for a quack who undertook to poison Sepher Bey on condition of receiving forty purses. When all was settled, the miscreant set out for Berat, and was immediately accused by Ali of evasion, and his wife and children were arrested as accomplices and detained, apparently as hostages for the good behaviour of their husband and father, but really as pledges for his silence when the crime should have been accomplished. Sepher Bey, informed of this by letters which Ali wrote to the Pacha of Berat demanding the fugitive, thought that a man persecuted by his enemy would be faithful to himself, and took the supposed runaway into his service. The traitor made skilful use of the kindness of his too credulous protector, insinuated himself into his confidence, became his trusted physician and apothecary, and gave him poison instead of medicine on the very first appearance of indisposition. As soon as symptoms of death appeared, the poisoner fled, aided by the emissaries of Ali, with whom the court of Berat was packed, and presented himself at Janina to receive the reward of his crime. Ali thanked him for his zeal, commended his skill, and referred him to the treasurer. But the instant the wretch left the seraglio in order to receive his recompense, he was seized by the executioners and hurried to the gallows. In thus punishing the assassin, Ali at one blow discharged the debt he owed him, disposed of the single witness to be dreaded, and displayed his own friendship for the victim! Not content with this, he endeavoured to again throw suspicion on the wife of Ibrahim Pacha, whom he accused of being jealous of the influence which Sepher Pacha had exercised in the family. This he mentioned regularly in conversation, writing in the same style to his agents at Constantinople, and everywhere where there was any profit in slandering a family whose ruin he desired for the sake of their possessions. Before long he made a pretext out of the scandal started by himself, and prepared to take up arms in order, he said, to avenge his friend Sepher Bey, when he was anticipated by Ibrahim Pacha, who roused against him the allied Christians of Thesprotia, foremost among whom ranked the Suliots famed through Albania for their courage and their love of independence.

After several battles, in which his enemies had the advantage, Ali began negotiations with Ibrahim, and finally concluded a treaty offensive and defensive. This fresh alliance was, like the first, to be cemented by a marriage. The virtuous Emineh, seeing her son Veli united to the second daughter of Ibrahim, trusted that the feud between the two families was now quenched, and thought herself at the summit of happiness. But her joy was not of long duration; the death-groan was again to be heard amidst the songs of the marriage-feast.

The daughter of Chainitza, by her first husband, Ali had married a certain Murad, the Bey of Clerisoura. This nobleman, attached to Ibrahim Pacha by both blood and affection, since the death of Sepher Bey, had, become the special object of Ali's hatred, caused by the devotion of Murad to his patron, over whom he had great influence, and from whom nothing could detach him. Skilful in concealing truth under special pretexts, Ali gave out that the cause of his known dislike to this young man was that the latter, although his nephew by marriage, had several times fought in hostile ranks against him. Therefore the amiable Ibrahim made use of the marriage treaty to arrange an honourable reconciliation between Murad Bey and his uncle, and appointed the former "Ruler of the Marriage Feast," in which capacity he was charged to conduct the bride to Janina and deliver her to her husband, the young Veli Bey. He had accomplished his mission satisfactorily, and was received by Ali with all apparent hospitality. The festival began on his arrival towards the end of November 1791, and had already continued several days, when suddenly it was announced that a shot had been fired upon Ali, who had only escaped by a miracle, and that the assassin was still at large. This news spread terror through the city and the palace, and everyone dreaded being seized as the guilty person. Spies were everywhere employed, but they declared search was useless, and that there must be an extensive conspiracy against Ali's life. The latter complained of being surrounded by enemies, and announced that henceforth he would receive only one person at a time, who should lay down his arms before entering the hall now set apart for public audience. It was a chamber built over a vault, and entered by a sort of trap-door, only reached by a ladder.

After having for several days received his couriers in this sort of dovecot, Ali summoned his nephew in order to entrust with him the wedding gifts. Murad took this as a sign of favour, and joyfully acknowledged the congratulations of his friends. He presented himself at the time arranged; the guards at the foot of the ladder demanded his arms, which he gave up readily, and ascended the ladder full of hope. Scarcely had the trap-door closed behind him when a pistol ball, fired from a dark corner, broke his shoulder blade, and he fell, but sprang up and attempted to fly. Ali issued from his hiding place and sprang upon him, but notwithstanding his wound the young bey defended himself vigorously, uttering terrible cries. The pacha, eager to finish, and finding his hands insufficient, caught a burning log from the hearth, struck his nephew in the face with it, felled him to the ground, and completed his bloody task. This accomplished, Ali called for help with loud cries, and when his guards entered he showed the bruises he had received and the blood with which he was covered, declaring that he had killed in self-defence a villain who endeavoured to assassinate him. He ordered the body to be searched, and a letter was found in a pocket which Ali had himself just placed there, which purported to give the details of the pretended conspiracy.

As Murad's brother was seriously compromised by this letter, he also was immediately seized, and strangled without any pretence of trial. The whole palace rejoiced, thanks were rendered to Heaven by one of those sacrifices of animals still occasionally made in the East to celebrate an escape from great danger, and Ali released some prisoners in order to show his gratitude to Providence for having protected him from so horrible a crime. He received congratulatory visits, and composed an apology attested by a judicial declaration by the cadi, in which the memory of Murad and his brother was declared accursed. Finally, commissioners, escorted by a strong body of soldiers, were sent to seize the property of the two brothers, because, said the decree, it was just that the injured should inherit the possessions of his would-be assassins.

Thus was exterminated the only family capable of opposing the Pacha of Janina, or which could counterbalance his influence over the weak Ibrahim of Berat. The latter, abandoned by his brave defenders, and finding himself at the mercy of his enemy, was compelled to submit to what he could not prevent, and protested only by tears against these crimes, which seemed to herald a terrible future for himself.

As for Emineh, it is said that from the date of this catastrophe she separated herself almost entirely from her blood-stained husband, and spent her life in the recesses of the harem, praying as a Christian both for the murderer and his victims. It is a relief, in the midst of this atrocious saturnalia to encounter this noble and gentle character, which like a desert oasis, affords a rest to eyes wearied with the contemplation of so much wickedness and treachery.

Ali lost in her the guardian angel who alone could in any way restrain his violent passions. Grieved at first by the withdrawal of the wife whom hitherto he had loved exclusively, he endeavoured in vain to regain her affection; and then sought in new vices compensation for the happiness he had lost, and gave himself up to sensuality. Ardent in everything, he carried debauchery to a monstrous extent, and as if his palaces were not large enough for his desires, he assumed various disguises; sometimes in order to traverse the streets by night in search of the lowest pleasures; sometimes penetrating by day into churches and private houses seeking for young men and maidens remarkable for their beauty, who were then carried off to his harem.

His sons, following in his footsteps, kept also scandalous households, and seemed to dispute preeminence in evil with their father, each in his own manner. Drunkenness was the specialty of the eldest, Mouktar, who was without rival among the hard drinkers of Albania, and who was reputed to have emptied a whole wine-skin in one evening after a plentiful meal. Gifted with the hereditary violence of his family, he had, in his drunken fury, slain several persons, among others his sword-bearer, the companion of his childhood and confidential friend of his whole life. Veli chose a different course. Realising the Marquis de Sade, as his father had realised Macchiavelli, he delighted in mingling together debauchery and cruelty, and his amusement consisted in biting the lips he had kissed, and tearing with his nails the forms he had caressed. The people of Janina saw with horror more than one woman in their midst whose nose and ears he had caused to be cut off, and had then turned into the streets.

It was indeed a reign of terror; neither fortune, life, honour, nor family were safe. Mothers cursed their fruitfulness, and women their beauty. Fear soon engenders corruption, and subjects are speedily tainted by the depravity of their masters. Ali, considering a demoralised race as easier to govern, looked on with satisfaction.

While he strengthened by every means his authority from within, he missed no opportunity of extending his rule without. In 1803 he declared war against the Suliots, whose independence he had frequently endeavoured either to purchase or to overthrow. The army sent against them, although ten thousand strong, was at first beaten everywhere. Ali then, as usual, brought treason to his aid, and regained the advantage. It became evident that, sooner or later, the unhappy Suliots must succumb.

Foreseeing the horrors which their defeat would entail, Emineh, touched with compassion, issued from her seclusion and cast herself at Ali's feet. He raised her, seated her beside him, and inquired as to her wishes. She spoke of generosity, of mercy; he listened as if touched and wavering, until she named the Suliots. Then, filled with fury, he seized a pistol and fired at her. She was not hurt, but fell to the ground overcome with terror, and her women hastily intervened and carried her away. For the first time in his life, perhaps, Ali shuddered before the dread of a murder.

It was his wife, the mother of his children, whom he saw lying at his feet, and the recollection afflicted and tormented him. He rose in the night and went to Emineh's apartment; he knocked and called, but being refused admittance, in his anger he broke open the door. Terrified by the noise; and at the sight of her infuriated husband, Emineh fell into violent convulsions, and shortly expired. Thus perished the daughter of Capelan Pacha, wife of Ali Tepeleni, and mother of Mouktar and Veli, who, doomed to live surrounded by evil, yet remained virtuous and good.

Her death caused universal mourning throughout Albania, and produced a not less deep impression on the mind of her murderer. Emineh's spectre pursued him in his pleasures, in the council chamber, in the hours of night. He saw her, he heard her, and would awake, exclaiming, "my wife! my wife! – It is my wife! – Her eyes are angry; she threatens me! – Save me! Mercy!" For more than ten years Ali never dared to sleep alone.

IV

In December, the Suliots, decimated by battle, worn by famine, discouraged by treachery, were obliged to capitulate. The treaty gave them leave to go where they would, their own mountains excepted. The unfortunate tribe divided into two parts, the one going towards Parga, the other towards Prevesa. Ali gave orders for the destruction of both, notwithstanding the treaty.

The Parga division was attacked in its march, and charged by a numerous body of Skipetars. Its destruction seemed imminent, but instinct suddenly revealed to the ignorant mountaineers the one manoeuvre which might save them. They formed a square, placing old men, women, children, and cattle in the midst, and, protected by this military formation, entered Parga in full view of the cut-throats sent to pursue them.

Less fortunate was the Prevesa division, which, terrified by a sudden and unexpected attack, fled in disorder to a Greek convent called Zalongos. But the gate was soon broken down, and the unhappy Suliots massacred to the last man.

The women, whose tents had been pitched on the summit of a lofty rock, beheld the terrible carnage which destroyed their defenders. Henceforth their only prospect was that of becoming the slaves of those who had just slaughtered their husbands and brothers. An heroic resolution spared them this infamy; they joined hands, and chanting their national songs, moved in a solemn dance round the rocky platform. As the song ended, they uttered a prolonged and piercing cry, and cast themselves and their children down into the profound abyss beneath.

There were still some Suliots left in their country when Ali Pacha took possession of it. These were all taken and brought to Janina, and their sufferings were the first adornments of the festival made for the army. Every soldier's imagination was racked for the discovery of new tortures, and the most original among them had the privilege of themselves carrying out their inventions.

There were some who, having had their noses and ears cut off, were compelled to eat them raw, dressed as a salad. One young man was scalped until the skin fell back upon his shoulders, then beaten round the court of the seraglio for the pacha's entertainment, until at length a lance was run through his body and he was cast on the funeral pile. Many were boiled alive and their flesh then thrown to the dogs.

From this time the Cross has disappeared from the Selleid mountains, and the gentle prayer of Christ no longer wakes the echoes of Suli.

During the course of this war, and shortly after the death of Emineh, another dismal drama was enacted in the pacha's family, whose active wickedness nothing seemed to weary. The scandalous libertinism of both father and sons had corrupted all around as well as themselves. This demoralisation brought bitter fruits for all alike: the subjects endured a terrible tyranny; the masters sowed among themselves distrust, discord, and hatred. The father wounded his two sons by turns in their tenderest affections, and the sons avenged themselves by abandoning their father in the hour of danger.

There was in Janina a woman named Euphrosyne, a niece of the archbishop, married to one of the richest Greek merchants, and noted for wit and beauty. She was already the mother of two children, when Mouktar became enamoured of her, and ordered her to come to his palace. The unhappy Euphrosyne, at once guessing his object, summoned a family council to decide what should be done. All agreed that there was no escape, and that her husband's life was in danger, on account of the jealousy of his terrible rival. He fled the city that same night, and his wife surrendered herself to Mouktar, who, softened by her charms, soon sincerely loved her, and overwhelmed her with presents and favours. Things were in this position when Mouktar was obliged to depart on an important expedition.

Scarcely had he started before his wives complained to Ali that Euphrosyne usurped their rights and caused their husband to neglect them. Ali, who complained greatly of his sons' extravagance, and regretted the money they squandered, at once struck a blow which was both to enrich himself and increase the terror of his name.

One night he appeared by torchlight, accompanied by his guards, at Euphrosyne's house. Knowing his cruelty and avarice, she sought to disarm one by gratifying the other: she collected her money and jewels and laid them at Ali's feet with a look of supplication.

"These things are only my own property, which you restore," said he, taking possession of the rich offering. "Can you give back the heart of Mouktar, which you have stolen?"

Euphrosyne besought him by his paternal feelings, for the sake of his son whose love had been her misfortune and was now her only crime, to spare a mother whose conduct had been otherwise irreproachable. But her tears and pleadings produced no effect on Ali, who ordered her to be taken, loaded with fetters and covered with a piece of sackcloth, to the prison of the seraglio.

If it were certain that there was no hope for the unhappy Euphrosyne, one trusted that she might at least be the only victim. But Ali, professing to follow the advice of some severe reformers who wished to restore decent morality, arrested at the same time fifteen ladies belonging to the best Christian families in Janina. A Wallachian, named Nicholas Janco, took the opportunity to denounce his own wife, who was on the point of becoming a mother, as guilty of adultery, and handed her also over to the pacha. These unfortunate women were brought before Ali to undergo a trial of which a sentence of death was the foregone conclusion. They were then confined in a dungeon, where they spent two days of misery. The third night, the executioners appeared to conduct them to the lake where they were to perish. Euphrosyne, too exhausted to endure to the end, expired by the way, and when she was flung with the rest into the dark waters, her soul had already escaped from its earthly tenement. Her body was found the next day, and was buried in the cemetery of the monastery of Saints-Anargyres, where her tomb, covered with white iris and sheltered by a wild olive tree, is yet shown.

Mouktar was returning from his expedition when a courier from his brother Veli brought him a letter informing him of these events. He opened it. "Euphrosyne!" he cried, and, seizing one of his pistols, fired it at the messenger, who fell dead at his feet, – "Euphrosyne, behold thy first victim!" Springing on his horse, he galloped towards Janina. His guards followed at a distance, and the inhabitants of all the villages he passed fled at his approach. He paid no attention to them, but rode till his horse fell dead by the lake which had engulfed Euphrosyne, and then, taking a boat, he went to hide his grief and rage in his own palace.

Ali, caring little for passion which evaporated in tears and cries, sent an order to Mouktar to appear before him at once. "He will not kill you," he remarked to his messenger, with a bitter smile. And, in fact, the man who a moment before was furiously raging and storming against his father, as if overwhelmed by this imperious message, calmed down, and obeyed.

"Come hither, Mouktar," said the pacha, extending his murderous hand to be kissed as soon as his son appeared. "I shall take no notice of your anger, but in future never forget that a man who braves public opinion as I do fears nothing in the world. You can go now; when your troops have rested from their march, you can come and ask for orders. Go, remember what I have said."

Mouktar retired as submissively as if he had just received pardon for some serious crime, and found no better consolation than to spend the night with Veli in drinking and debauchery. But a day was to come when the brothers, alike outraged by their father, would plot and carry out a terrible vengeance.

However, the Porte began to take umbrage at the continual aggrandisement of the Pacha of Janina. Not daring openly to attack so formidable a vassal, the sultan sought by underhand means to diminish his power, and under the pretext that Ali was becoming too old for the labour of so many offices, the government of Thessaly was withdrawn from him, but, to show that this was not done in enmity, the province was entrusted to his nephew, Elmas Bey, son of Suleiman and Chainitza.

Chainitza, fully as ambitious as her brother, could not contain her delight at the idea of governing in the name of her son, who was weak and gentle in character and accustomed to obey her implicitly. She asked her brother's permission to go to Trikala to be present at the installation, and obtained it, to everybody's astonishment; for no one could imagine that Ali would peacefully renounce so important a government as that of Thessaly. However, he dissembled so skilfully that everyone was deceived by his apparent resignation, and applauded his magnanimity, when he provided his sister with a brilliant escort to conduct her to the capital of the province of which he had just been deprived in favour of his nephew. He sent letters of congratulation to the latter as well as magnificent presents, among them a splendid pelisse of black fox, which had cost more than a hundred thousand francs of Western money. He requested Elmas Bey to honour him by wearing this robe on the day when the sultan's envoy should present him with the firman of investiture, and Chainitza herself was charged to deliver both gifts and messages.

Chainitza arrived safely at Trikala, and faithfully delivered the messages with which she had been entrusted. When the ceremony she so ardently desired took place, she herself took charge of all the arrangements. Elmas, wearing the black fox pelisse, was proclaimed, and acknowledged as Governor of Thessaly in her presence. "My son is pacha!" she cried in the delirium of joy. "My son is pacha! and my nephews will die of envy!" But her triumph was not to be of long duration. A few days after his installation, Elmas began to feel strangely languid. Continual lethargy, convulsive sneezing, feverish eyes, soon betokened a serious illness. Ali's gift had accomplished its purpose. The pelisse, carefully impregnated with smallpox germs taken from a young girl suffering from this malady, had conveyed the dreaded disease to the new pacha, who, not having been inoculated, died in a few days.

The grief of Chainitza at her son's death displayed itself in sobs, threats, and curses, but, not knowing whom to blame for her misfortune, she hastened to leave the scene of it, and returned to Janina, to mingle her tears with those of her brother. She found Ali apparently in such depths of grief, that instead of suspecting, she was actually tempted to pity him, and this seeming sympathy soothed her distress, aided by the caresses of her second son, Aden Bey. Ali, thoughtful of his own interests, took care to send one of his own officers to Trikala, to administer justice in the place of his deceased nephew, and the Porte, seeing that all attempts against him only caused misfortune, consented to his resuming the government of Thessaly.

This climax roused the suspicions of many persons. But the public voice, already discussing the causes of the death of Elmas, was stifled by the thunder of the cannon, which, from the ramparts of Janina, announced to Epirus the birth of another son to Ali, Salik Bey, whose mother was a Georgian slave.

Fortune, seemingly always ready both to crown Ali's crimes with success and to fulfil his wishes, had yet in reserve a more precious gift than any of the others, that of a good and beautiful wife who should replace, and even efface the memory of the beloved Emineh.

The Porte, while sending to Ali the firman which restored to him the government of Thessaly, ordered him to seek out and destroy a society of coiners who dwelt within his jurisdiction. Ali, delighted to prove his zeal by a service which cost nothing but bloodshed, at once set his spies to work, and having discovered the abode of the gang, set out for the place attended by a strong escort. It was a village called Plikivitza.

Having arrived in the evening, he spent the night in taking measures to prevent escape, and at break of day attacked the village suddenly with his whole force. The coiners were seized in the act. Ali immediately ordered the chief to be hung at his own door and the whole population to be massacred. Suddenly a young girl of great beauty made her way through the tumult and sought refuge at his feet. Ali, astonished, asked who she was. She answered with a look of mingled innocence and terror, kissing his hands, which she bathed with tears, and said:

"O my lord! I implore thee to intercede with the terrible vizier Ali for my mother and brothers. My father is dead, behold where he hangs at the door of our cottage! But we have done nothing to rouse the anger of our dreadful master. My mother is a poor woman who never offended anyone, and we are only weak children. Save us from him!"

Touched in spite of himself, the pacha took the girl in his arms, and answered her with a gentle smile.

"Thou hast come to the wrong man, child: I am this terrible vizier."

"Oh no, no! you are good, you will be our good lord."

"Well, be comforted, my child, and show me thy mother and thy brothers; they shall be spared. Thou hast saved their lives."

And as she knelt at his feet, overcome with joy, he raised her and asked her name.

"Basilessa," she replied.

"Basilessa, Queen! it is a name of good augury. Basilessa, thou shalt dwell with me henceforth."

And he collected the members of her family, and gave orders for them to be sent to Janina in company with the maiden, who repaid his mercy with boundless love and devotion.

Let us mention one trait of gratitude shown by Ali at the end of this expedition, and his record of good deeds is then closed. Compelled by a storm to take refuge in a miserable hamlet, he inquired its name, and on hearing it appeared surprised and thoughtful, as if trying to recall lost memories. Suddenly he asked if a woman named Nouza dwelt in the village, and was told there was an old infirm woman of that name in great poverty. He ordered her to be brought before him. She came and prostrated herself in terror. Ali raised her kindly.

"Dost thou not know me?" he asked.

"Have mercy, great Vizier," answered the poor woman, who, having nothing to lose but her life, imagined that even that would be taken from her.

"I see," said the pacha, "that if thou knowest me, thou dost not really recognise me."

The woman looked at him wonderingly, not understanding his words in the least.

"Dost thou remember," continued Ali, "that forty years ago a young man asked for shelter from the foes who pursued him? Without inquiring his name or standing, thou didst hide him in thy humble house, and dressed his wounds, and shared thy scanty food with him, and when he was able to go forward thou didst stand on thy threshold to wish him good luck and success. Thy wishes were heard, for the young man was Ali Tepeleni, and I who speak am he!"

The old woman stood overwhelmed with astonishment. She departed calling down blessings on the pacha, who assured her a pension of fifteen hundred francs for the rest of her days.

But these two good actions are only flashes of light illuminating the dark horizon of Ali's life for a brief moment. Returned to Janina, he resumed his tyranny, his intrigues, and cruelty. Not content with the vast territory which owned his sway, he again invaded that of his neighbours on every pretext. Phocis, Mtolia, Acarnania, were by turns occupied by his troops, the country ravaged, and the inhabitants decimated. At the same time he compelled Ibrahim Pacha to surrender his last remaining daughter, and give her in marriage to his nephew, Aden Bey, the son of Chainitza. This new alliance with a family he had so often attacked and despoiled gave him fresh arms against it, whether by being enabled better to watch the pacha's sons, or to entice them into some snare with greater ease.

Whilst he thus married his nephew, he did not neglect the advancement of his sons. By the aid of the French Ambassador, whom he had convinced of his devotion to the Emperor Napoleon, he succeeded in getting the pachalik of Morea bestowed on Veli, and that of Lepanto on Mouktar. But as in placing his sons in these exalted positions his only aim was to aggrandise and consolidate his own power, he himself ordered their retinues, giving them officers of his own choosing. When they departed to their governments, he kept their wives, their children, and even their furniture as pledges, saying that they ought not to be encumbered with domestic establishments in time of war, Turkey just then being at open war with England. He also made use of this opportunity to get rid of people who displeased him; among others, of a certain Ismail Pacho Bey, who had been alternately both tool and enemy, whom he made secretary to his son Veli, professedly as a pledge of reconciliation and favour, but really in order to despoil him more easily of the considerable property which he possessed at Janina. Pacho was not deceived, and showed his resentment openly. "The wretch banishes me," he cried, pointing out Ali, who was sitting at a window in the palace; "he sends me away in order to rob me; but I will avenge myself whatever happens, and I shall die content if I can procure his destruction at the price of my own."

Continually increasing his power, Ali endeavoured to consolidate it permanently. He had entered by degrees into secret negotiations with all the great powers of Europe, hoping in the end to make himself independent, and to obtain recognition as Prince of Greece. A mysterious and unforeseen incident betrayed this to the Porte, and furnished actual proofs of his treason in letters confirmed by Ali's own seal. The Sultan Selim immediately sent to Janina a "kapidgi-bachi," or plenipotentiary, to examine into the case and try the delinquent.

Arrived at Janina, this officer placed before Ali the proofs of his understanding with the enemies of the State. Ali was not strong enough to throw off the mask, and yet could not deny such overwhelming evidence. He determined to obtain time.

"No wonder," said he, "that I appear guilty in the eyes of His Highness. This seal is certainly mine; I cannot deny it; but the writing is not that of my secretaries, and the seal must have been obtained and used to sign these guilty letters in order to ruin me. I pray you to grant me a few days in order to clear up this iniquitous mystery, which compromises me in the eyes of my master the sultan and of all good Mahommedans. May Allah grant me the means of proving my innocence, which is as pure as the rays of the sun, although everything seems against me!"

After this conference, Ali, pretending to be engaged in a secret inquiry, considered how he could legally escape from this predicament. He spent some days in making plans which were given up as soon as formed, until his fertile genius at length suggested a means of getting clear of one of the greatest difficulties in which he had ever found himself. Sending for a Greek whom he had often employed, he addressed him thus:

"Thou knowest I have always shown thee favour, and the day is arrived when thy fortune shall be made. Henceforth thou shalt be as my son; thy children shall be as mine; my house shall be thy home, and in return for my benefits I require one small service. This accursed kapidgi-bachi has come hither bringing certain papers signed with my seal, intending to use them to my discredit, and thus to extort money from me. Of money I have already given too much, and I intend this time to escape without being plundered except for the sake of a good servant like thee. Therefore, my son, thou shalt go before the tribunal when I tell thee, and declare before this kapidgi-bachi and the cadi that thou hast written these letters attributed to me, and that thou didst seal them with my seal, in order to give them due weight and importance."

The unhappy Greek grew pale and strove to answer.

"What fearest thou, my son?" resumed Ali. "Speak, am I not thy good master? Thou wilt be sure of my lasting favour, and who is there to dread when I protect thee? Is it the kapidgi-bachi? he has no authority here. I have thrown twenty as good as he into the lake! If more is required to reassure thee, I swear by the Prophet, by my own and my sons' heads, that no harm shall come to thee from him. Be ready, then, to do as I tell thee, and beware of mentioning this matter to anyone, in order that all may be accomplished according to our mutual wishes."

More terrified by dread of the pacha, from whose wrath in case of refusal there was no chance of escape, than tempted by his promises, the Greek undertook the false swearing required. Ali, delighted, dismissed him with a thousand assurances of protection, and then requested the presence of the sultan's envoy, to whom he said, with much emotion:

"I have at length unravelled the infernal plot laid against me; it is the work of a man in the pay of the implacable enemies of the Sublime Porte, and who is a Russian agent. He is in my power, and I have given him hopes of pardon on condition of full confession. Will you then summon the cadi, the judges and ecclesiastics of the town, in order that they may hear the guilty man's deposition, and that the light of truth may purify their minds?"

The tribunal was soon assembled, and the trembling Greek appeared in the midst of a solemn silence. "Knowest thou this writing?" demanded the cadi. – "It is mine." – "And this seal?" – "It is that of my master, Ali Pacha." – "How does it come to be placed at the foot of these letters?" – "I did this by order of my chief, abusing the confidence of my master, who occasionally allowed me to use it to sign his orders." – "It is enough: thou canst withdraw."

Uneasy as to the success of his intrigue, Ali was approaching the Hall of Justice. As he entered the court, the Greek, who had just finished his examination, threw himself at his feet, assuring him that all had gone well. "It is good," said Ali; "thou shalt have thy reward." Turning round, he made a sign to his guards, who had their orders, and who instantly seized the unhappy Greek, and, drowning his voice with their shouts, hung him in the courtyard. This execution finished, the pacha presented himself before the judges and inquired the result of their investigation. He was answered by a burst of congratulation. "Well," said he, "the guilty author of this plot aimed at me is no more; I ordered him to be hung without waiting to hear your decision. May all enemies of our glorious sultan perish even as he!"

A report of what had occurred was immediately drawn up, and, to assist matters still further, Ali sent the kapidgi-bachi a gift of fifty purses, which he accepted without difficulty, and also secured the favour of the Divan by considerable presents. The sultan, yielding to the advice of his councillors, appeared to have again received him into favour.

But Ali knew well that this appearance of sunshine was entirely deceptive, and that Selim only professed to believe in his innocence until the day should arrive when the sultan could safely punish his treason. He sought therefore to compass the latter's downfall, and made common cause with his enemies, both internal and external. A conspiracy, hatched between the discontented pachas and the English agents, shortly broke out, and one day, when Ali was presiding at the artillery practice of some French gunners sent to Albania by the Governor of Illyria, a Tartar brought him news of the deposition of Selim, who was succeeded by his nephew Mustapha. Ali sprang up in delight, and publicly thanked Allah for this great good fortune. He really did profit by this change of rulers, but he profited yet more by a second revolution which caused the deaths both of Selim, whom the promoters wished to reestablish on the throne, and of Mustapha, whose downfall they intended. Mahmoud II, who was next invested with the scimitar of Othman, came to the throne in troublous times, after much bloodshed, in the midst of great political upheavals, and had neither the will nor the power to attack one of his most powerful vassals. He received with evident satisfaction the million piastres which, at his installation, Ali hastened to send as a proof of his devotion, assured the pacha of his favour, and confirmed both him and his sons in their offices and dignities. This fortunate change in his position brought Ali's pride and audacity to a climax. Free from pressing anxiety, he determined to carry out a project which had been the dream of his life.

V

After taking possession of Argyro-Castron, which he had long coveted, Ali led his victorious army against the town of Kardiki, whose inhabitants had formerly joined with those of Kormovo in the outrage inflicted on his mother and sister. The besieged, knowing they had no mercy to hope for, defended themselves bravely, but were obliged to yield to famine. After a month's blockade, the common people, having no food for themselves or their cattle, began to cry for mercy in the open streets, and their chiefs, intimidated by the general misery and unable to stand alone, consented to capitulate. Ali, whose intentions as to the fate of this unhappy town were irrevocably decided, agreed to all that they asked. A treaty was signed by both parties, and solemnly sworn to on the Koran, in virtue of which seventy-two beys, heads of the principal Albanian families, were to go to Janina as free men, and fully armed. They were to be received with the honours due to their rank as free tenants of the sultan, their lives and their families were to be spared, and also their possessions. The other inhabitants of Kardiki, being Mohammedans, and therefore brothers of Ali, were to be treated as friends and retain their lives and property. On these conditions a quarter of the town; was to be occupied by the victorious troops.

One of the principal chiefs, Saleh Bey, and his wife, foreseeing the fate which awaited their friends, committed suicide at the moment when, in pursuance of the treaty, Ali's soldiers took possession of the quarter assigned to them.

Ali received the seventy-two beys with all marks of friendship when they arrived at Janina. He lodged them in a palace on the lake, and treated them magnificently for some days. But soon, having contrived on some pretext to disarm them, he had them conveyed, loaded with chains, to a Greek convent on an island in the lake, which was converted into a prison. The day of vengeance not having fully arrived, he explained this breach of faith by declaring that the hostages had attempted to escape.

The popular credulity was satisfied by this explanation, and no one doubted the good faith of the pacha when he announced that he was going to Kardiki to establish a police and fulfil the promises he had made to the inhabitants. Even the number of soldiers he took excited no surprise, as Ali was accustomed to travel with a very numerous suite.

After three days' journey, he stopped at Libokhovo, where his sister had resided since the death of Aden Bey, her second son, cut off recently by wickness. What passed in the long interview they had no one knew, but it was observed that Chainitza's tears, which till then had flowed incessantly, stopped as if by magic, and her women, who were wearing mourning, received an order to attire themselves as for a festival. Feasting and dancing, begun in Ali's honour, did not cease after his departure.

He spent the night at Chenderia, a castle built on a rock, whence the town of Kardiki was plainly visible. Next day at daybreak Ali despatched an usher to summon all the male inhabitants of Kardiki to appear before Chenderia, in order to receive assurances of the pacha's pardon and friendship.

The Kardikiotes at once divined that this injunction was the precursor of a terrible vengeance: the whole town echoed with cries and groans, the mosques were filled with people praying for deliverance. The appointed time arrived, they embraced each other as if parting for ever, and then the men, unarmed, in number six hundred and seventy, started for Chenderia. At the gate of the town they encountered a troop of Albanians, who followed as if to escort them, and which increased in number as they proceeded. Soon they arrived in the dread presence of Ali Pacha. Grouped in formidable masses around him stood several thousand of his fierce soldiery.

The unhappy Kardikiotes realised their utter helplessness, and saw that they, their wives and children, were completely at the mercy of their implacable enemy. They fell prostrate before the pacha, and with all the fervour which the utmost terror could inspire, implored him to grant them a generous pardon.

Ali for some time silently enjoyed the pleasure of seeing his ancient enemies lying before him prostrate in the dust. He then desired them to rise, reassured them, called them brothers, sons, friends of his heart. Distinguishing some of his old acquaintances, he called them to him, spoke familiarly of the days of their youth, of their games, their early friendships, and pointing to the young men, said, with tears in his eyes,

"The discord which has divided us for so many years has allowed children not born at the time of our dissension to grow into men. I have lost the pleasure of watching the development of the off-spring of my neighbours and the early friends of my youth, and of bestowing benefits on them, but I hope shortly to repair the natural results of our melancholy divisions."

He then made them splendid promises, and ordered them to assemble in a neighbouring caravanserai, where he wished to give them a banquet in proof of reconciliation. Passing from the depths of despair to transports of joy, the Kardikiotes repaired gaily to the caravanserai, heaping blessings on the pacha, and blaming each other for having ever doubted his good faith.

Ali was carried down from Chenderia in a litter, attended by his courtiers, who celebrated his clemency in pompous speeches, to which he replied with gracious smiles. At the foot of the steep descent he mounted his horse, and, followed by his troops, rode towards the caravanserai. Alone, and in silence, he rode twice round it, then, returning to the gate, which had just been closed by his order, he pulled up his horse, and, signing to his own bodyguard to attack the building, "Slay them!" he cried in a voice of thunder.

The guards remained motionless in surprise and horror, then as the pacha, with a roar, repeated his order, they indignantly flung down their arms. In vain he harangued, flattered, or threatened them; some preserved a sullen silence, others ventured to demand mercy. Then he ordered them away, and, calling on the Christian Mirdites who served under his banner.

"To you, brave Latins," he cried, "I will now entrust the duty of exterminating the foes of my race. Avenge me, and I will reward you magnificently."

A confused murmur rose from the ranks. Ali imagined they were consulting as to what recompense should be required as the price of such deed.

"Speak," said he; "I am ready to listen to your demands and to satisfy them."

Then the Mirdite leader came forward and threw back the hood of his black cloak.

"O Pacha!" said he, looking Ali boldly in the face, "thy words are an insult; the Mirdites do not slaughter unarmed prisoners in cold blood. Release the Kardikiotes, give them arms, and we will fight them to the death; but we serve thee as soldiers and not as executioners."

At these words; which the black-cloaked battalion received with applause, Ali thought himself betrayed, and looked around with doubt and mistrust. Fear was nearly taking the place of mercy, words of pardon were on his lips, when a certain Athanasius Vaya, a Greek schismatic, and a favourite of the pacha's, whose illegitimate son he was supposed to be, advanced at the head of the scum of the army, and offered to carry out the death sentence. Ali applauded his zeal, gave him full authority to act, and spurred his horse to the top of a neighbouring hill, the better to enjoy the spectacle. The Christian Mirdites and the Mohammedan guards knelt together to pray for the miserable Kardikiotes, whose last hour had come.

The caravanserai where they were shut in was a square enclosure, open to the sky, and intended to shelter herds of buffaloes. The prisoners having heard nothing of what passed outside, were astonished to behold Athanasius Vaya and his troop appearing on the top of the wall. They did not long remain in doubt. Ali gave the signal by a pistol-shot, and a general fusillade followed. Terrible cries echoed from the court; the prisoners, terrified, wounded, crowded one upon another for shelter. Some ran frantically hither and thither in this enclosure with no shelter and no exit, until they fell, struck down by bullets. Some tried to climb the walls, in hope of either escape or vengeance, only to be flung back by either scimitars or muskets. It was a terrible scene of despair and death.

After an hour of firing, a gloomy silence descended on the place, now occupied solely by a heap of corpses. Ali forbade any burial rites on pain of death, and placed over the gate an inscription in letters of gold, informing posterity that six hundred Kardikiotes had there been sacrificed to the memory of his mother Kamco.

When the shrieks of death ceased in the enclosure, they began to be heard in the town. The assassins spread themselves through it, and having violated the women and children, gathered them into a crowd to be driven to Libokovo. At every halt in this frightful journey fresh marauders fell on the wretched victims, claiming their share in cruelty and debauchery. At length they arrived at their destination, where the triumphant and implacable Chainitza awaited them. As after the taking of Kormovo, she compelled the women to cut off their hair and to stuff with it a mattress on which she lay. She then stripped them, and joyfully narrated to them the massacre of their husbands, fathers, brothers and sons, and when she had sufficiently enjoyed their misery they were again handed over to the insults of the soldiery. Chainitza finally published an edict forbidding either clothes, shelter, or food to be given to the women and children of Kardiki, who were then driven forth into the woods either to die of hunger or to be devoured by wild beasts. As to the seventy-two hostages, Ali put them all to death when he returned to Janina. His vengeance was indeed complete.

But as, filled with a horrible satisfaction, the pacha was enjoying the repose of a satiated tiger, an indignant and threatening voice reached him even in the recesses of his palace. The Sheik Yussuf, governor of the castle of Janina, venerated as a saint by the Mohammedans on account of his piety, and universally beloved and respected for his many virtues, entered Ali's sumptuous dwelling for the first time. The guards on beholding him remained stupefied and motionless, then the most devout prostrated themselves, while others went to inform the pacha; but no one dared hinder the venerable man, who walked calmly and solemnly through the astonished attendants. For him there existed no antechamber, no delay; disdaining the ordinary forms of etiquette, he paced slowly through the various apartments, until, with no usher to announce him, he reached that of Ali. The latter, whose impiety by no means saved him from superstitious terrors, rose hastily from the divan and advanced to meet the holy sheik, who was followed by a crowd of silent courtiers. Ali addressed him with the utmost respect, and endeavoured even to kiss his right hand. Yussuf hastily withdrew it, covered it with his mantle, and signed to the pacha to seat himself. Ali mechanically obeyed, and waited in solemn silence to hear the reason of this unexpected visit.

Yussuf desired him to listen with all attention, and then reproached him for his injustice and rapine, his treachery and cruelty, with such vivid eloquence that his hearers dissolved in tears. Ali, though much dejected, alone preserved his equanimity, until at length the sheik accused him of having caused the death of Emineh. He then grew pale, and rising, cried with terror:

"Alas! my father, whose name do you now pronounce? Pray for me, or at least do not sink me to Gehenna with your curses!"

"There is no need to curse thee," answered Yussuf. "Thine own crimes bear witness against thee. Allah has heard their cry. He will summon thee, judge thee, and punish thee eternally. Tremble, for the time is at hand! Thine hour is coming – is coming – is coming!"

Casting a terrible glance at the pacha, the holy man turned his back on him, and stalked out of the apartment without another word.

Ali, in terror, demanded a thousand pieces of gold, put them in a white satin purse, and himself hastened with them to overtake the sheik, imploring him to recall his threats. But Yussuf deigned no answer, and arrived at the threshold of the palace, shook off the dust of his feet against it.

Ali returned to his apartment sad and downcast, and many days elapsed before he could shake off the depression caused by this scene. But soon he felt more ashamed of his inaction than of the reproaches which had caused it, and on the first opportunity resumed his usual mode of life.

The occasion was the marriage of Moustai, Pacha of Scodra, with the eldest daughter of Veli Pacha, called the Princess of Aulis, because she had for dowry whole villages in that district. Immediately after the announcement of this marriage Ali set on foot a sort of saturnalia, about the details of which there seemed to be as much mystery as if he had been preparing an assassination.

All at once, as if by a sudden inundation, the very scum of the earth appeared to spread over Janina. The populace, as if trying to drown their misery, plunged into a drunkenness which simulated pleasure. Disorderly bands of mountebanks from the depths of Roumelia traversed the streets, the bazaars and public places; flocks and herds, with fleeces dyed scarlet, and gilded horns, were seen on all the roads driven to the court by peasants under the guidance of their priests. Bishops, abbots, ecclesiastics generally, were compelled to drink, and to take part in ridiculous and indecent dances, Ali apparently thinking to raise himself by degrading his more respectable subjects. Day and night these spectacles succeeded each other with increasing rapidity, the air resounded with firing, songs, cries, music, and the roaring of wild beasts in shows. Enormous spits, loaded with meat, smoked before huge braziers, and wine ran in floods at tables prepared in the palace courts. Troops of brutal soldiers drove workmen from their labour with whips, and compelled them to join in the entertainments; dirty and impudent jugglers invaded private houses, and pretending that they had orders from the pacha to display their skill, carried boldly off whatever they could lay their hands upon. Ali saw the general demoralization with pleasure, especially as it tended to the gratification of his avarice. Every guest was expected to bring to the palace gate a gift in proportion to his means, and foot officers watched to see that no one forgot this obligation. At length, on the nineteenth day, Ali resolved to crown the feast by an orgy worthy of himself. He caused the galleries and halls of his castle by the lake to be decorated with unheard-of splendour, and fifteen hundred guests assembled for a solemn banquet. The pacha appeared in all his glory, surrounded by his noble attendants and courtiers, and seating himself on a dais raised above this base crowd which trembled at his glance, gave the signal to begin. At his voice, vice plunged into its most shameless diversions, and the wine-steeped wings of debauchery outspread themselves over the feast. All tongues were at their freest, all imaginations ran wild, all evil passions were at their height, when suddenly the noise ceased, and the guests clung together in terror. A man stood at the entrance of the hall, pale, disordered, and wild-eyed, clothed in torn and blood-stained garments. As everyone made way at his approach, he easily reached the pacha, and prostrating himself at his feet, presented a letter. Ali opened and rapidly perused it; his lips trembled, his eyebrows met in a terrible frown, the muscles of his forehead contracted alarmingly. He vainly endeavoured to smile and to look as if nothing had happened, his agitation betrayed him, and he was obliged to retire, after desiring a herald to announce that he wished the banquet to continue.

Now for the subject of the message, and the cause of the dismay it produced.

VI

Ali had long cherished a violent passion for Zobeide, the wife of his son Veli Pacha. Having vainly attempted to gratify it after his son's departure, and being indignantly repulsed, he had recourse to drugs, and the unhappy Zobeide remained in ignorance of her misfortune until she found she was pregnant. Then, half-avowals from her women, compelled to obey the pacha from fear of death, mixed with confused memories of her own, revealed the whole terrible truth. Not knowing in her despair which way to turn, she wrote to Ali, entreating him to visit the harem. As head of the family, he had a right to enter, being supposed responsible for the conduct of his sons' families, no-law-giver having hitherto contemplated the possibility of so disgraceful a crime. When he appeared, Zobeide flung herself at his feet, speechless with grief. Ali acknowledged his guilt, pleaded the violence of his passion, wept with his victim, and entreating her to control herself and keep silence, promised that all should be made right. Neither the prayers nor tears of Zobeide could induce him to give up the intention of effacing the traces of his first crime by a second even more horrible.

But the story was already whispered abroad, and Pacho Bey learnt all its details from the spies he kept in Janina. Delighted at the prospect of avenging himself on the father, he hastened with his news to the son. Veli Pacha, furious, vowed vengeance, and demanded Pacho Bey's help, which was readily promised. But Ali had been warned, and was not a man to be taken unawares. Pacho Bey, whom Veli had just promoted to the office of sword-bearer, was attacked in broad daylight by six emissaries sent from Janina. He obtained timely help, however, and five of the assassins, taken red-handed, were at once hung without ceremony in the market-place. The sixth was the messenger whose arrival with the news had caused such dismay at Ali's banquet.

As Ali reflected how the storm he had raised could best be laid, he was informed that the ruler of the marriage feast sent by Moustai, Pacha of Scodra, to receive the young bride who should reign in his harem, had just arrived in the plain of Janina. He was Yussuf Bey of the Delres, an old enemy of Ali's, and had encamped with his escort of eight hundred warriors at the foot of Tomoros of Dodona. Dreading some treachery, he absolutely refused all entreaties to enter the town, and Ali seeing that it was useless to insist, and that his adversary for the present was safe, at once sent his grand-daughter, the Princess of Aulis, out to him.

This matter disposed of, Ali was able to attend to his hideous family tragedy. He began by effecting the disappearance of the women whom he had been compelled to make his accomplices; they were simply sewn up in sacks by gipsies and thrown into the lake. This done, he himself led the executioners into a subterranean part of the castle, where they were beheaded by black mutes as a reward for their obedience. He then sent a doctor to Zobeide; who succeeded in causing a miscarriage, and who, his work done, was seized and strangled by the black mutes who had just beheaded the gipsies. Having thus got rid of all who could bear witness to his crime, he wrote to Veli that he might now send for his wife and two of his children, hitherto detained as hostages, and that the innocence of Zobeide would confound a calumniator who had dared to assail him with such injurious suspicions.

When this letter arrived, Pacho Bey, distrusting equally the treachery of the father and the weakness of the son, and content with having sown the seeds of dissension in his enemy's family, had sufficient wisdom to seek safety in flight. Ali, furious, vowed, on hearing this, that his vengeance should overtake him even at the ends of the earth. Meanwhile he fell back on Yussuf Bey of the Debres, whose escape when lately at Janina still rankled in his mind. As Yussuf was dangerous both from character and influence, Ali feared to attack him openly, and sought to assassinate him. This was not precisely easy, for, exposed to a thousand dangers of this kind, the nobles of that day were on their guard. Steel and poison were used up, and another way had to be sought. Ali found it.

One of the many adventurers with whom Janina was filled penetrated to the pacha's presence, and offered to sell the secret of a powder whereof three grains would suffice to kill a man with a terrible explosion – explosive powder, in short. Ali heard with delight, but replied that he must see it in action before purchasing.

In the dungeons of the castle by the lake, a poor monk of the order of St. Basil was slowly dying, for having boldly refused a sacrilegious simony proposed to him by Ali. He was a fit subject for the experiment, and was successfully blown to pieces, to the great satisfaction of Ali, who concluded his bargain, and hastened to make use of it. He prepared a false firman, which, according to custom, was enclosed and sealed in a cylindrical case, and sent to Yussuf Bey by a Greek, wholly ignorant of the real object of his mission. Opening it without suspicion, Yussuf had his arm blown off, and died in consequence, but found time to despatch a message to Moustai Pacha of Scodra, informing him of the catastrophe, and warning him to keep good guard.

Yussuf's letter was received by Moustai just as a similar infernal machine was placed in his hands under cover to his young wife. The packet was seized, and a careful examination disclosed its nature. The mother of Moustai, a jealous and cruel woman, accused her daughter-in-law of complicity, and the unfortunate Ayesha, though shortly to become a mother, expired in agony from the effects of poison, only guilty of being the innocent instrument of her grandfather's treachery.

Fortune, having frustrated Ali's schemes concerning Moustai Pacha, offered him as consolation a chance of invading the territory of Parga, the only place in Epirus which had hitherto escaped his rule, and which he greedily coveted. Agia, a small Christian town on the coast, had rebelled against him and allied itself to Parga. It provided an excuse for hostilities, and Ali's troops, under his son Mouktar, first seized Agia, where they only found a few old men to massacre, and then marched on Parga, where the rebels had taken refuge. After a few skirmishes, Mouktar entered the town, and though the Parganiotes fought bravely, they must inevitably have surrendered had they been left to themselves. But they had sought protection from the French, who had garrisoned the citadel, and the French grenadiers descending rapidly from the height, charged the Turks with so much fury that they fled in all directions, leaving on the field four "bimbashis," or captains of a thousand, and a considerable number of killed and wounded.

The pacha's fleet succeeded no better than his army. Issuing from the Gulf of Ambracia, it was intended to attack Parga from the sea, joining in the massacre, and cutting off all hope of escape from that side, Ali meaning to spare neither the garrison nor any male inhabitants over twelve years of age. But a few shots fired from a small fort dispersed the ships, and a barque manned by sailors from Paxos pursued them, a shot from which killed Ali's admiral on his quarter-deck. He was a Greek of Galaxidi, Athanasius Macrys by name.

Filled with anxiety, Ali awaited news at Prevesa, where a courier, sent off at the beginning of the action, had brought him oranges gathered in the orchards of Parga. Ali gave him a purse of gold, and publicly proclaimed his success. His joy was redoubled when a second messenger presented two heads of French soldiers, and announced that his troops were in possession of the lower part of Parga. Without further delay he ordered his attendants to mount, entered his carriage, and started triumphantly on the Roman road to Nicopolis. He sent messengers to his generals, ordering them to spare the women and children of Parga, intended for his harem, and above all to take strict charge of the plunder. He was approaching the arena of Nicopolis when a third Tartar messenger informed him of the defeat of his army. Ali changed countenance, and could scarcely articulate the order to return to Prevesa. Once in his palace, he gave way to such fury that all around him trembled, demanding frequently if it could be true that his troops were beaten. "May your misfortune be upon us!" his attendants answered, prostrating themselves. All at once, looking out on the calm blue sea which lay before his windows, he perceived his fleet doubling Cape Pancrator and re-entering the Ambracian Gulf under full sail; it anchored close by the palace, and on hailing the leading ship a speaking trumpet announced to Ali the death of his admiral, Athanasius Macrys.

"But Parga, Parga!" cried Ali.

"May Allah grant the pacha long life! The Parganiotes have escaped the sword of His Highness."

"It is the will of Allah!" murmured the pacha; whose head sank upon his breast in dejection.

Arms having failed, Ali, as usual, took refuge in plots and treachery, but this time, instead of corrupting his enemies with gold, he sought to weaken them by division.

VII

The French commander Nicole, surnamed the "Pilgrim," on account of a journey he had once made to Mecca, had spent six months at Janina with a brigade of artillery which General Marmont, then commanding in the Illyrian provinces, had for a time placed at Ali's disposal. The old officer had acquired the esteem and friendship of the pacha, whose leisure he had often amused by stories of his campaigns and various adventures, and although it was now long since they had met, he still had the reputation of being Ali's friend. Ali prepared his plans accordingly. He wrote a letter to Colonel Nicole, apparently in continuation of a regular correspondence between them, in which he thanked the colonel for his continued affection, and besought him by various powerful motives to surrender Parga, of which he promised him the governorship during the rest of his life. He took good care to complete his treason by allowing the letter to fall into the hands of the chief ecclesiastics of Parga, who fell head-foremost into the trap. Seeing that the tone of the letter was in perfect accordance with the former friendly relations between their French governor and the pacha, they were convinced of the former's treachery. But the result was not as Ali had hoped: the Parganiotes resumed their former negotiations with the English, preferring to place their freedom in the hands of a Christian nation rather than to fall under the rule of a Mohammedan satrap.... The English immediately sent a messenger to Colonel Nicole, offering honourable conditions of capitulation. The colonel returned a decided refusal, and threatened to blow up the place if the inhabitants, whose intentions he guessed, made the slightest hostile movement. However, a few days later, the citadel was taken at night, owing to the treachery of a woman who admitted an English detachment; and the next day, to the general astonishment, the British standard floated over the Acropolis of Parga.

All Greece was then profoundly stirred by a faint gleam of the dawn of liberty, and shaken by a suppressed agitation. The Bourbons again reigned in France, and the Greeks built a thousand hopes on an event which changed the basis of the whole European policy. Above all, they reckoned on powerful assistance from Russia. But England had already begun to dread anything which could increase either the possessions or the influence of this formidable power. Above all, she was determined that the Ottoman Empire should remain intact, and that the Greek navy, beginning to be formidable, must be destroyed. With these objects in view, negotiations with Ali Pacha were resumed. The latter was still smarting under his recent disappointment, and to all overtures answered only, "Parga! I must have Parga." – And the English were compelled to yield it!

Trusting to the word of General Campbell, who had formally promised, on its surrender, that Parga should be classed along with the seven Ionian Isles; its grateful inhabitants were enjoying a delicious rest after the storm, when a letter from the Lord High Commissioner, addressed to Lieutenant-Colonel de Bosset, undeceived them, and gave warning of the evils which were to burst on the unhappy town.

On the 25th of March, 1817, notwithstanding the solemn promise made to the Parganiotes, when they admitted the British troops, that they should always be on the same footing as the Ionian Isles, a treaty was signed at Constantinople by the British Plenipotentiary, which stipulated the complete and stipulated cession of Parga and all its territory to the Ottoman Empire. Soon there arrived at Janina Sir John Cartwright, the English Consul at Patras, to arrange for the sale of the lands of the Parganiotes and discuss the conditions of their emigration. Never before had any such compact disgraced European diplomacy, accustomed hitherto to regard Turkish encroachments as simple sacrilege. But Ali Pacha fascinated the English agents, overwhelming them with favours, honours, and feasts, carefully watching them all the while. Their correspondence was intercepted, and he endeavoured by means of his agents to rouse the Parganiotes against them. The latter lamented bitterly, and appealed to Christian Europe, which remained deaf to their cries. In the name of their ancestors, they demanded the rights which had been guaranteed them. "They will buy our lands," they said; "have we asked to sell them? And even if we received their value, can gold give us a country and the tombs of our ancestors?"

Ali Pacha invited the Lord High Commissioner of Great Britain, Sir Thomas Maitland, to a conference at Prevesa, and complained of the exorbitant price of 1,500,000, at which the commissioners had estimated Parga and its territory, including private property and church furniture. It had been hoped that Ali's avarice would hesitate at this high price, but he was not so easily discouraged. He give a banquet for the Lord High Commissioner, which degenerated into a shameless orgy. In the midst of this drunken hilarity the Turk and the Englishman disposed of the territory of Parga; agreeing that a fresh estimate should be made on the spot by experts chosen by both English and Turks. The result of this valuation was that the indemnity granted to the Christians was reduced by the English to the sum of 276,075 sterling, instead of the original 500,000. And as Ali's agents only arrived at the sum of 56,750, a final conference was held at Buthrotum between Ali and the Lord High Commissioner. The latter then informed the Parganiotes that the indemnity allowed them was irrevocably fixed at 150,000! The transaction is a disgrace to the egotistical and venal nation which thus allowed the life and liberty of a people to be trifled with, a lasting blot on the honour of England!

The Parganiotes at first could believe neither in the infamy of their protectors nor in their own misfortune; but both were soon confirmed by a proclamation of the Lord High Commissioner, informing them that the pacha's army was marching to take possession of the territory which, by May 10th, must be abandoned for ever.

The fields were then in full bearing. In the midst of plains ripening for a rich harvest were 80,000 square feet of olive trees, alone estimated at two hundred thousand guineas. The sun shone in cloudless azure, the air was balmy with the scent of orange trees, of pomegranates and citrons. But the lovely country might have been inhabited by phantoms; only hands raised to heaven and brows bent to the dust met one's eye. Even the very dust belonged no more to the wretched inhabitants; they were forbidden to take a fruit or a flower, the priests might not remove either relics or sacred images. Church, ornaments, torches, tapers, pyxes, had by this treaty all become Mahommedan property. The English had sold everything, even to the Host! Two days more, and all must be left. Each was silently marking the door of the dwelling destined so soon to shelter an enemy, with a red cross, when suddenly a terrible cry echoed from street to street, for the Turks had been perceived on the heights overlooking the town. Terrified and despairing, the whole population hastened to fall prostrate before the Virgin of Parga, the ancient guardian of their citadel. A mysterious voice, proceeding from the sanctuary, reminded them that the English had, in their iniquitous treaty, forgotten to include the ashes of those whom a happier fate had spared the sight of the ruin of Parga. Instantly they rushed to the graveyards, tore open the tombs, and collected the bones and putrefying corpses. The beautiful olive trees were felled, an enormous funeral pyre arose, and in the general excitement the orders of the English chief were defied. With naked daggers in their hands, standing in the crimson light of the flames which were consuming the bones of their ancestors, the people of Parga vowed to slay their wives and children, and to kill themselves to the last man, if the infidels dared to set foot in the town before the appointed hour. Xenocles, the last of the Greek poets, inspired by this sublime manifestation of despair, even as Jeremiah by the fall of Jerusalem, improvised a hymn which expresses all the grief of the exiles, and which the exiles interrupted by their tears and sobs.

A messenger, crossing the sea in all haste, informed the Lord High Commissioner of the terrible threat of the Parganiotes. He started at once, accompanied by General Sir Frederic Adams, and landed at Parga by the light of the funeral pyre. He was received with ill-concealed indignation, and with assurances that the sacrifice would be at once consummated unless Ali's troops were held back. The general endeavoured to console and to reassure the unhappy people, and then proceeded to the outposts, traversing silent streets in which armed men stood at each door only waiting a signal before slaying their families, and then turning their weapons against the English and themselves. He implored them to have patience, and they answered by pointing to the approaching Turkish army and bidding him hasten. He arrived at last and commenced negotiations, and the Turkish officers, no less uneasy than the English garrison, promised to wait till the appointed hour. The next day passed in mournful silence, quiet as death. At sunset on the following day, May 9, 1819, the English standard on the castle of Parga was hauled down, and after a night spent in prayer and weeping, the Christians demanded the signal of departure.

They had left their dwellings at break of day, and, scattering on the shore, endeavoured to collect some relics of their country. Some filled little bags with ashes withdrawn from the funeral pile; others took handfuls of earth, while the women and children picked up pebbles which they hid in their clothing and pressed to their bosoms, as if fearing to be deprived of them. Meanwhile, the ships intended to transport them arrived, and armed English soldiers superintended the embarkation, which the Turks hailed from afar with ferocious cries. The Parganiotes were landed in Corfu, where they suffered yet more injustice. Under various pretexts the money promised them was reduced and withheld, until destitution compelled them to accept the little that was offered. Thus closed one of the most odious transactions which modern history has been compelled to record.

The satrap of Janina had arrived at the fulfilment of his wishes. In the retirement of his fairy-like palace by the lake he could enjoy voluptuous pleasures to the full. But already seventy-eight years had passed over his head, and old age had laid the burden of infirmity upon him. His dreams were dreams of blood, and vainly he sought refuge in chambers glittering with gold, adorned with arabesques, decorated with costly armour and covered with the richest of Oriental carpets; remorse stood ever beside him. Through the magnificence which surrounded him there constantly passed the pale spectre of Emineh, leading onwards a vast procession of mournful phantoms, and the guilty pacha buried his face in his hands and shrieked aloud for help. Sometimes, ashamed of his weakness, he endeavoured to defy both the reproaches of his conscience and the opinion of the multitude, and sought to encounter criticism with bravado. If, by chance, he overheard some blind singer chanting in the streets the satirical verses which, faithful to the poetical and mocking genius of their ancestors, the Greeks frequently composed about him, he would order the singer to be brought, would bid him repeat his verses, and, applauding him, would relate some fresh anecdote of cruelty, saying, "Go, add that to thy tale; let thy hearers know what I can do; let them understand that I stop at nothing in order to overcome my foes! If I reproach myself with anything, it is only with the deeds I have sometimes failed to carry out."

Sometimes it was the terrors of the life after death which assailed him. The thought of eternity brought terrible visions in its train, and Ali shuddered at the prospect of Al-Sirat, that awful bridge, narrow as a spider's thread and hanging over the furnaces of Hell which a Mussulman must cross in order to arrive at the gate of Paradise. He ceased to joke about Eblis, the Prince of Evil, and sank by degrees into profound superstition. He was surrounded by magicians and soothsayers; he consulted omens, and demanded talismans and charms from the dervishes, which he had either sewn into his garments, or suspended in the most secret parts of his palace, in order to avert evil influences. A Koran was hung about his neck as a defence against the evil eye, and frequently he removed it and knelt before it, as did Louis XI before the leaden figures of saints which adorned his hat. He ordered a complete chemical laboratory from Venice, and engaged alchemists to distill the water of immortality, by the help of which he hoped to ascend to the planets and discover the Philosophers' Stone. Not perceiving any practical result of their labours, he ordered the laboratory to be burnt and the alchemists to be hung.

Ali hated his fellow-men. He would have liked to leave no survivors, and often regretted his inability to destroy all those who would have cause to rejoice at his death. Consequently he sought to accomplish as much harm as he could during the time which remained to him, and, for no possible reason but that of hatred, he caused the arrest of both Ibrahim pacha, who had already suffered so much at his hands, and his son, and confined them both in a dungeon purposely constructed under the grand staircase of the castle by the lake, in order that he might have the pleasure of passing over their heads each time he left his apartments or returned to them.

It was not enough for Ali merely to put to death those who displeased him; the form of punishment must be constantly varied in order to produce a fresh mode of suffering, therefore new tortures had to be constantly invented. Now it was a servant, guilty of absence without leave, who was bound to a stake in the presence of his sister, and destroyed by a cannon placed six paces off, but only loaded with powder, in order to prolong the agony; now, a Christian accused of having tried to blow up Janina by introducing mice with tinder fastened to their tails into the powder magazine, who was shut up in the cage of Ali's favourite tiger and devoured by it.

The pacha despised the human race as much as he hated it. A European having reproached him with the cruelty shown to his subjects, Ali replied: –

"You do not understand the race with which I have to deal. Were I to hang a criminal on yonder tree, the sight would not deter even his own brother from stealing in the crowd at its foot. If I had an old man burnt alive, his son would steal the ashes and sell them. The rabble can be governed by fear only, and I am the one man who does it successfully."

His conduct perfectly corresponded to his ideas. One great feast-day, two gipsies devoted their lives in order to avert the evil destiny of the pacha; and, solemnly convoking on their own heads all misfortunes which might possibly befall him, cast themselves down from the palace roof. One arose with difficulty, stunned and suffering, the other remained on the ground with a broken leg. Ali gave them each forty francs and an annuity of two pounds of maize daily, and considering this sufficient, took no further trouble about them.

Every year, at Ramadan, a large sum was distributed in alms among poor women without distinction of sect. But Ali contrived to change this act of benevolence into a barbarous form of amusement.

As he possessed several palaces in Janina at a considerable distance from each other, the one at which a distribution was to take place was each day publicly announced, and when the women had waited there for an hour or two, exposed to sun, rain or cold, as the case might be, they were suddenly informed that they must go to some other palace, at the opposite end of the town. When they got there, they usually had to wait for another hour, fortunate if they were not sent off to a third place of meeting. When the time at length arrived, an eunuch appeared, followed by Albanian soldiers armed with staves, carrying a bag of money, which he threw by handfuls right into the midst of the assembly. Then began a terrible uproar. The women rushed to catch it, upsetting each other, quarreling, fighting, and uttering cries of terror and pain, while the Albanians, pretending to enforce order, pushed into the crowd, striking right and left with their batons. The pacha meanwhile sat at a window enjoying the spectacle, and impartially applauding all well delivered blows, no matter whence they came. During these distributions, which really benefitted no one, many women were always severely hurt, and some died from the blows they had received.

Ali maintained several carriages for himself and his family, but allowed no one else to share in this prerogative. To avoid being jolted, he simply took up the pavement in Janina and the neighbouring towns, with the result that in summer one was choked by dust, and in winter could hardly get through the mud. He rejoiced in the public inconvenience, and one day having to go out in heavy rain, he remarked to one of the officers of his escort, "How delightful to be driven through this in a carriage, while you will have the pleasure of following on horseback! You will be wet and dirty, whilst I smoke my pipe and laugh at your condition."

He could not understand why Western sovereigns should permit their subjects to enjoy the same conveniences and amusements as themselves. "If I had a theatre," he said, "I would allow no one to be present at performances except my own children; but these idiotic Christians do not know how to uphold their own dignity."

There was no end to the mystifications which it amused the pacha to carry out with those who approached him.

One day he chose to speak Turkish to a Maltese merchant who came to display some jewels. He was informed that the merchant understood only Greek and Italian. He none the less continued his discourse without allowing anyone to translate what he said into Greek. The Maltese at length lost patience, shut up his cases, and departed. Ali watched him with the utmost calm, and as he went out told him, still in Turkish, to come again the next day.

An unexpected occurrence seemed, like the warning finger of Destiny, to indicate an evil omen for the pacha's future. "Misfortunes arrive in troops," says the forcible Turkish proverb, and a forerunner of disasters came to Ali Pacha.

One morning he was suddenly roused by the Sheik Yussuf, who had forced his way in, in spite of the guards. "Behold!" said he, handing Ali a letter, "Allah, who punishes the guilty, has permitted thy seraglio of Tepelen to be burnt. Thy splendid palace, thy beautiful furniture, costly stuffs, cashmeers, furs, arms, all are destroyed! And it is thy youngest and best beloved son, Salik Bey himself, whose hand kindled the flames!" So saying, Yussuf turned and departed, crying with a triumphant voice, "Fire! fire! fire!"

Ali instantly ordered his horse, and, followed by his guards, rode without drawing rein to Tepelen. As soon as he arrived at the place where his palace had formerly insulted the public misery, he hastened to examine the cellars where his treasures were deposited. All was intact, silver plate, jewels, and fifty millions of francs in gold, enclosed in a well over which he had caused a tower to be built. After this examination he ordered all the ashes to be carefully sifted in hopes of recovering the gold in the tassels and fringes of the sofas, and the silver from the plate and the armour. He next proclaimed through the length and breadth of the land, that, being by the hand of Allah deprived of his house, and no longer possessing anything in his native town, he requested all who loved him to prove their affection by bringing help in proportion. He fixed the day of reception for each commune, and for almost each individual of any rank, however small, according to their distance from Tepelen, whither these evidences of loyalty were to be brought.

During five days Ali received these forced benevolences from all parts. He sat, covered with rags, on a shabby palm-leaf mat placed at the outer gate of his ruined palace, holding in his left hand a villainous pipe of the kind used by the lowest people, and in his right an old red cap, which he extended for the donations of the passers-by. Behind stood a Jew from Janina, charged with the office of testing each piece of gold and valuing jewels which were offered instead of money; for, in terror, each endeavoured to appear generous. No means of obtaining a rich harvest were neglected; for instance, Ali distributed secretly large sums among poor and obscure people, such as servants, mechanics, and soldiers, in order that by returning them in public they might appear to be making great sacrifices, so that richer and more distinguished persons could not, without appearing ill-disposed towards the pacha, offer only the same amount as did the poor, but were obliged to present gifts of enormous value.

After this charity extorted from their fears, the pacha's subjects hoped to be at peace. But a new decree proclaimed throughout Albania required them to rebuild and refurnish the formidable palace of Tepelen entirely at the public expense. Ali then returned to Janina, followed by his treasure and a few women who had escaped from the flames, and whom he disposed of amongst his friends, saying that he was no longer sufficiently wealthy to maintain so many slaves.

Fate soon provided him with a second opportunity for amassing wealth. Arta, a wealthy town with a Christian population, was ravaged by the plague, and out of eight thousand inhabitants, seven thousand were swept away. Hearing this, Ali hastened to send commissioners to prepare an account of furniture and lands which the pacha claimed as being heir to his subjects. A few livid and emaciated spectres were yet to be found in the streets of Arta. In order that the inventory might be more complete, these unhappy beings were compelled to wash in the Inachus blankets, sheets, and clothes steeped in bubonic infection, while the collectors were hunting everywhere for imaginary hidden treasure. Hollow trees were sounded, walls pulled down, the most unlikely corners examined, and a skeleton which was discovered still girt with a belt containing Venetian sequins was gathered up with the utmost care. The archons of the town were arrested and tortured in the hope of discovering buried treasure, the clue to which had disappeared along with the owners. One of these magistrates, accused of having hidden some valuable objects, was plunged up to his shoulders in a boiler full of melted lead and boiling oil. Old men, women, children, rich and poor alike, were interrogated, beaten, and compelled to abandon the last remains of their property in order to save their lives.

Having thus decimated the few inhabitants remaining to the town, it became necessary to repeople it. With this object in view, Ali's emissaries overran the villages of Thessaly, driving before them all the people they met in flocks, and compelling them to settle in Arta. These unfortunate colonists were also obliged to find money to pay the pacha for the houses they were forced to occupy.

This business being settled, Ali turned to another which had long been on his mind. We have seen how Ismail Pacho Bey escaped the assassins sent to murder him. A ship, despatched secretly from Prevesa, arrived at the place of his retreat. The captain, posing as a merchant, invited Ismail to come on board and inspect his goods. But the latter, guessing a trap, fled promptly, and for some time all trace of him was lost. Ali, in revenge, turned his wife out of the palace at Janina which she still occupied, and placed her in a cottage, where she was obliged to earn a living by spinning. But he did not stop there, and, learning after some time that Pacho Bey had sought refuge with the Nazir of Drama, who had taken him into favour, he resolved to strike a last blow, more sure and more terrible than the others. Again Ismail's lucky star saved him from the plots of his enemy. During a hunting party he encountered a kapidgi-bachi, or messenger from the sultan, who asked him where he could find the Nazir, to whom he was charged with an important communication. As kapidgi-bachis are frequently bearers of evil tidings, which it is well to ascertain at once, and as the Nazir was at some distance, Pacho Bey assumed the latter's part, and the sultan's confidential messenger informed him that he was the bearer of a firman granted at the request of Ali Pacha of Janina.

"Ali of Tepeleni. He is my friend. How can I serve him?"

"By executing the present order, sent you by the Divan, desiring you to behead a traitor, named Pacho Bey, who crept into your service a short time ago."

"Willingly! but he is not an easy man to seize being brave, vigorous, clever, and cunning. Craft will be necessary in this case. He may appear at any moment, and it is advisable that he should not see you. Let no one suspect who you are, but go to Drama, which is only two hours distant, and await me there. I shall return this evening, and you can consider your errand as accomplished."

The kapidgi-bachi made a sign of comprehension, and directed his course towards Drama; while Ismail, fearing that the Nazir, who had only known him a short time, would sacrifice him with the usual Turkish indifference, fled in the opposite direction. At the end of an hour he encountered a Bulgarian monk, with whom he exchanged clothes – a disguise which enabled him to traverse Upper Macedonia in safety. Arriving at the great Servian convent in the mountains whence the Axius takes its rise, he obtained admission under an assumed name. But feeling sure of the discretion of the monks, after a few days he explained his situation to them.

Ali, learning the ill-success of his latest stratagem, accused the Nazir of conniving at Pacho Bey's escape. But the latter easily justified himself with the Divan by giving precise information of what had really occurred. This was what Ali wanted, who profited thereby in having the fugitive's track followed up, and soon got wind of his retreat. As Pacho Bey's innocence had been proved in the explanations given to the Porte, the death firman obtained against him became useless, and Ali affected to abandon him to his fate, in order the better to conceal the new plot he was conceiving against him.

Athanasius Vaya, chief assassin of the Kardikiotes, to whom Ali imparted his present plan for the destruction of Ismail, begged for the honour of putting it into execution, swearing that this time Ismail should not escape. The master and the instrument disguised their scheme under the appearance of a quarrel, which astonished the whole town. At the end of a terrible scene which took place in public, Ali drove the confidant of his crimes from the palace, overwhelming him with insults, and declaring that were Athanasius not the son of his children's foster-mother, he would have sent him to the gibbet. He enforced his words by the application of a stick, and Vaya, apparently overwhelmed by terror and affliction, went round to all the nobles of the town, vainly entreating them to intercede for him. The only favour which Mouktar Pacha could obtain for him was a sentence of exile allowing him to retreat to Macedonia.

Athanasius departed from Janina with all the demonstrations of utter despair, and continued his route with the haste of one who fears pursuit. Arrived in Macedonia, he assumed the habit of a monk, and undertook a pilgrimage to Mount Athos, saying that both the disguise and the journey were necessary to his safety. On the way he encountered one of the itinerant friars of the great Servian convent, to whom he described his disgrace in energetic terms, begging him to obtain his admission among the lay brethren of his monastery.

Delighted at the prospect of bringing back to the fold of the Church a man so notorious for his crimes, the friar hastened to inform his superior, who in his turn lost no time in announcing to Pacho Bey that his compatriot and companion in misfortune was to be received among the lay brethren, and in relating the history of Athanasius as he himself had heard it. Pacho Bey, however, was not easily deceived, and at once guessing that Vaya's real object was his own assassination, told his doubts to the superior, who had already received him as a friend. The latter retarded the reception of Vaya so as to give Pacho time to escape and take the road to Constantinople. Once arrived there, he determined to brave the storm and encounter Ali openly.

Endowed by nature with a noble presence and with masculine firmness, Pacho Bey possessed also the valuable gift of speaking all the various tongues of the Ottoman Empire. He could not fail to distinguish himself in the capital and to find an opening for his great talents. But his inclination drove him at first to seek his fellow-exiles from Epirus, who were either his old companions in arms, friends, or relations, for he was allied to all the principal families, and was even, through his wife, nearly connected with his enemy, Ali Pacha himself.

He had learnt what this unfortunate lady had already endured on his account, and feared that she would suffer yet more if he took active measures against the pacha. While he yet hesitated between affection and revenge, he heard that she had died of grief and misery. Now that despair had put an end to uncertainty, he set his hand to the work.

At this precise moment Heaven sent him a friend to console and aid him in his vengeance, a Christian from AEtolia, Paleopoulo by name. This man was on the point of establishing himself in Russian Bessarabia, when he met Pacho Bey and joined with him in the singular coalition which was to change the fate of the Tepelenian dynasty.

Paleopoulo reminded his companion in misfortune of a memorial presented to the Divan in 1812, which had brought upon Ali a disgrace from which he only escaped in consequence of the overwhelming political events which just then absorbed the attention of the Ottoman Government. The Grand Seigneur had sworn by the tombs of his ancestors to attend to the matter as soon as he was able, and it was only requisite to remind him of his vow. Pacho Bey and his friend drew up a new memorial, and knowing the sultan's avarice, took care to dwell on the immense wealth possessed by Ali, on his scandalous exactions, and on the enormous sums diverted from the Imperial Treasury. By overhauling the accounts of his administration, millions might be recovered. To these financial considerations Pacho Bey added some practical ones. Speaking as a man sure of his facts and well acquainted with the ground, he pledged his head that with twenty thousand men he would, in spite of Ali's troops and strongholds, arrive before Janina without firing a musket.

However good these plans appeared, they were by no means to the taste of the sultan's ministers, who were each and all in receipt of large pensions from the man at whom they struck. Besides, as in Turkey it is customary for the great fortunes of Government officials to be absorbed on their death by the Imperial Treasury, it of course appeared easier to await the natural inheritance of Ali's treasures than to attempt to seize them by a war which would certainly absorb part of them. Therefore, while Pacho Bey's zeal was commended, he obtained only dilatory answers, followed at length by a formal refusal.

Meanwhile, the old AEtolian, Paleopoulo, died, having prophesied the approaching Greek insurrection among his friends, and pledged Pacho Bey to persevere in his plans of vengeance, assuring him that before long Ali would certainly fall a victim to them. Thus left alone, Pacho, before taking any active steps in his work of vengeance, affected to give himself up to the strictest observances of the Mohammedan religion. Ali, who had established a most minute surveillance over his actions, finding that his time was spent with ulemas and dervishes, imagined that he had ceased to be dangerous, and took no further trouble about him.

VIII

A career of successful crime had established Ali's rule over a population equal to that of the two kingdoms of Sweden and Norway. But his ambition was not yet satisfied. The occupation of Parga did not crown his desires, and the delight which it caused him was much tempered by the escape of the Parganiotes, who found in exile a safe refuge from his persecution. Scarcely had he finished the conquest of Middle Albania before he was exciting a faction against the young Moustai Pacha in Scodra, a new object of greed. He also kept an army of spies in Wallachia, Moldavia, Thrace, and Macedonia, and, thanks to them, he appeared to be everywhere present, and was mixed up in every intrigue, private or political, throughout the empire. He had paid the English agents the price agreed on for Parga, but he repaid himself five times over, by gifts extorted from his vassals, and by the value of the Parga lands, now become his property. His palace of Tepelen had been rebuilt at the public expense, and was larger and more magnificent than before; Janina was embellished with new buildings; elegant pavilions rose on the shores of the lake; in short, Ali's luxury was on a level with his vast riches. His sons and grandsons were provided for by important positions, and Ali himself was sovereign prince in everything but the name.

There was no lack of flattery, even from literary persons. At Vienna a poem was printed in his honour, and a French-Greek Grammar was dedicated to him, and such titles as "Most Illustrious," "Most Powerful," and "Most Clement," were showered upon him, as upon a man whose lofty virtues and great exploits echoed through the world. A native of Bergamo, learned in heraldry, provided him with a coat of arms, representing, on a field gules, a lion, embracing three cubs, emblematic of the

Tepelenian dynasty. Already he had a consul at Leucadia accepted by the English, who, it is said, encouraged him to declare himself heredi- tary Prince of Greece, under the nominal suzerainty of the sultan; their real intention being to use him as a tool in return for their protection, and to employ him as a political counter-balance to the hospodars of Moldavia and Wallachia, who for the last twenty years had been simply Russian agents in disguise. This was not all; many of the adventurers with whom the Levant swarms, outlaws from every country, had found a refuge in Albania, and helped not a little to excite Ali's ambition by their suggestions. Some of these men frequently saluted him as King, a title which he affected to reject with indignation; and he disdained to imitate other states by raising a private standard of his own, preferring not to compromise his real power by puerile displays of dignity; and he lamented the foolish ambition of his children, who would ruin him, he said, by aiming, each, at becoming a vizier. Therefore he did not place his hope or confidence in them, but in the adventurers of every sort and kind, pirates, coiners, renegades, assassins, whom he kept in his pay and regarded as his best support. These he sought to attach to his person as men who might some day be found useful, for he did not allow the many favours of fortune to blind him to the real danger of his position. "A vizier," he was answered, "resembles a man wrapped in costly furs, but he sits on a barrel of powder, which only requires a spark to explode it." The Divan granted all the concessions which Ali demanded, affecting ignorance of his projects of revolt and his intelligence with the enemies of the State; but then apparent weakness was merely prudent temporis- ing. It was considered that Ali, already advanced in years, could not live much longer, and it was hoped that, at his death, Continental Greece, now in some measure detached from the Ottoman rule, would again fall under the sultan's sway.

Meanwhile, Pacho Bey, bent on silently undermining Ali's influence, had established himself as an intermediary for all those who came to de- mand justice on account of the pacha's exactions, and he contrived that both his own complaints and those of his clients should penetrate to the ears of the sultan, who, pitying his misfortunes, made him a kapidgi- bachi, as a commencement of better things. About this time the sultan also admitted to the Council a certain Abdi Effendi of Larissa, one of the richest nobles of Thessaly, who had been compelled by the tyranny of Veli Pacha to fly from his country. The two new dignitaries, having secured Khalid Effendi as a partisan, resolved to profit by his influence to carry out their plans of vengeance on the Tepelenian family. The news of Pacho Bey's promotion roused Ali from the security in which he was plunged, and he fell a prey to the most lively anxiety. Comprehending at once the evil which this man, – trained in his own school, – might cause him, he exclaimed, "Ah! if Heaven would only restore me the strength of my youth, I would plunge my sword into his heart even in the midst of the Divan."

It was not long before Ali's enemies found an extremely suitable opportunity for opening their attack. Veli Pacha, who had for his own profit increased the Thessalian taxation fivefold, had in doing so caused so much oppression that many of the inhabitants preferred the griefs and dangers of emigration rather than remain under so tyrannical a rule. A great number of Greeks sought refuge at Odessa, and the great Turkish families assembled round Pacho Bey and Abdi Effendi at Constantinople, who lost no opportunity of interceding in their favour. The sultan, who as yet did not dare to act openly against the Tepelenian family, was at least able to relegate Veli to the obscure post of Lepanto, and Veli, much disgusted, was obliged to obey. He quitted the new palace he had just built at Rapehani, and betook himself to the place of exile, accompanied by actors, Bohemian dancers, bear leaders, and a crowd of prostitutes.

Thus attacked in the person of his most powerful son, Ali thought to terrify his enemies by a daring blow. He sent three Albanians to Constantinople to assassinate Pacho Bey. They fell upon him as he was proceeding to the Mosque of Saint-Sophia, on the day on which the sultan also went in order to be present at the Friday ceremonial prayer, and fired several shots at him. He was wounded, but not mortally.

The assassins, caught red-handed, were hung at the gate of the Imperial Seraglio, but not before confessing that they were sent by the Pacha of Janina. The Divan, comprehending at last that so dangerous a man must be dealt with at any cost, recapitulated all Ali's crimes, and pronounced a sentence against him which was confirmed by a decree of the Grand Mufti. It set forth that Ali Tepelen, having many times obtained pardon for his crimes, was now guilty of high treason in the first degree, and that he would, as recalcitrant, be placed under the ban of the Empire if he did not within forty days appear at the Gilded Threshold of the Felicitous Gate of the Monarch who dispenses crowns to the princes who reign in this world, in order to justify himself. As may be supposed, submission to such an order was about the last thing Ali contemplated.

As he failed to appear, the Divan caused the Grand Mufti to launch the thunder of excommunication against him.

Ali had just arrived at Parga, which he now saw for the third time since he had obtained it, when his secretaries informed him that only the rod of Moses could save him from the anger of Pharaoh – a figurative mode of warning him that he had nothing to hope for. But Ali, counting on his usual luck, persisted in imagining that he could, once again, escape from his difficulty by the help of gold and intrigue. Without discontinuing the pleasures in which he was immersed, he contented himself with sending presents and humble petitions to Constantinople. But both were alike useless, for no one even ventured to transmit them to the sultan, who had sworn to cut off the head of anyone who dared mention the name of Ali Tepeleni in his presence.

Receiving no answer to his overtures, Ali became a prey to terrible anxiety. As he one day opened the Koran to consult it as to his future, his divining rod stopped at verse 82, chap. xix., which says, "He doth flatter himself in vain. He shall appear before our tribunal naked and bare." Ali closed the book and spat three times into his bosom. He was yielding to the most dire presentiments, when a courier, arriving from the capital, informed him that all hope of pardon was lost.

He ordered his galley to be immediately prepared, and left his seraglio, casting a look of sadness on the beautiful gardens where only yesterday he had received the homage of his prostrate slaves. He bade farewell to his wives, saying that he hoped soon to return, and descended to the shore, where the rowers received him with acclamations. The sail was set to a favourable breeze, and Ali, leaving the shore he was never to see again, sailed towards Erevesa, where he hoped to meet the Lord High Commissioner Maitland. But the time of prosperity had gone by, and the regard which had once been shown him changed with his fortunes. The interview he sought was not granted.

The sultan now ordered a fleet to be equipped, which, after Ramadan, was to disembark troops on the coast of Epirus, while all the neighbouring pachas received orders to hold themselves in readiness to march with all the troops of their respective Governments against Ali, whose name was struck out of the list of viziers. Pacho Bey was named pacha of Janina and Delvino on condition of subduing them, and was placed in command of the whole expedition.

However, notwithstanding these orders, there was not at the beginning of April, two months after the attempted assassination of Pacho Bey, a single soldier ready to march on Albania. Ramadan, that year, did not close until the new moon of July. Had Ali put himself boldly at the head of the movement which was beginning to stir throughout Greece, he might have baffled these vacillating projects, and possibly dealt a fatal blow to the Ottoman Empire. As far back as 1808, the Hydriotes had offered to recognise his son Veli, then Vizier of the Morea, as their Prince, and to support him in every way, if he would proclaim the independence of the Archipelago. The Moreans bore him no enmity until he refused to help them to freedom, and would have returned to him had he consented.

On the other side, the sultan, though anxious for war, would not spend a penny in order to wage it; and it was not easy to corrupt some of the great vassals ordered to march at their own expense against a man in whose downfall they had no special interest. Nor were the means of seduction wanting to Ali, whose wealth was enormous; but he preferred to keep it in order to carry on the war which he thought he could no longer escape. He made, therefore, a general appeal to all Albanian warriors, whatever their religion. Mussulmans and Christians, alike attracted by the prospect of booty and good pay, flocked to his standard in crowds.

He organised all these adventurers on the plan of the Armatous, by companies, placing a captain of his own choice at the head of each, and giving each company a special post to defend. Of all possible plans this was the best adapted to his country, where only a guerilla warfare can be carried on, and where a large army could not subsist.

In repairing to the posts assigned to them, these troops committed such terrible depredations that the provinces sent to Constantinople demanding their suppression. The Divan answered the petitioners that it was their own business to suppress these disorders, and to induce the Klephotes to turn their arms against Ali, who had nothing to hope from the clemency of the Grand Seigneur. At the same time circular letters were addressed to the Epirotes, warning them to abandon the cause of a rebel, and to consider the best means of freeing themselves from a traitor, who, having long oppressed them, now sought to draw down on their country all the terrors of war. Ali, who everywhere maintained numerous and active spies, now redoubled his watchfulness, and not a single letter entered Epirus without being opened and read by his agents. As an extra precaution, the guardians of the passes were enjoined to slay without mercy any despatch-bearer not provided with an order signed by Ali himself; and to send to Janina under escort any travellers wishing to enter Epirus. These measures were specially aimed against Suleyman Pacha, who had succeeded Veli in the government of Thessaly, and replaced Ali himself in the office of Grand Provost of the Highways. Suleyman's secretary was a Greek called Anagnorto, a native of Macedonia, whose estates Ali had seized, and who had fled with his family to escape further persecution. He had become attached to the court party, less for the sake of vengeance on Ali than to aid the cause of the Greeks, for whose freedom he worked by underhand methods. He persuaded Suleyman Pacha that the Greeks would help him to dethrone Ali, for whom they cherished the deepest hatred, and he was determined that they should learn the sentence of deprivation and excommunication fulminated against the rebel pacha. He introduced into the Greek translation which he was commissioned to make, ambiguous phrases which were read by the Christians as a call to take up arms in the cause of liberty. In an instant, all Hellas was up in arms. The Mohammedans were alarmed, but the Greeks gave out that it was in order to protect themselves and their property against the bands of brigands which had appeared on all sides. This was the beginning of the Greek insurrection, and occurred in May 1820, extending from Mount Pindus to Thermopylae. However, the Greeks, satisfied with having vindicated their right to bear arms in their own defence, continued to pay their taxes, and abstained from all hostility.

At the news of this great movement, Ali's friends advised him to turn it to his own advantage. "The Greeks in arms," said they, "want a chief: offer yourself as their leader. They hate you, it is true, but this feeling may change. It is only necessary to make them believe, which is easily done, that if they will support your cause you will embrace Christianity and give them freedom."

There was no time to lose, for matters became daily more serious. Ali hastened to summon what he called a Grand Divan, composed of the chiefs of both sects, Mussulmans and Christians. There were assembled men of widely different types, much astonished at finding themselves in company: the venerable Gabriel, Archbishop of Janina, and uncle of the unfortunate Euphrosyne, who had been dragged thither by force; Abbas, the old head of the police, who had presided at the execution of the Christian martyr; the holy bishop of Velas, still bearing the marks of the chains with which Ali had loaded him; and Porphyro, Archbishop of Arta, to whom the turban would have been more becoming than the mitre.

Ashamed of the part he was obliged to play, Ali, after long hesitation, decided on speaking, and, addressing the Christians, "O Greeks!" he said, "examine my conduct with unprejudiced minds, and you will see manifest proofs of the confidence and consideration which I have ever shown you. What pacha has ever treated you as I have done? Who would have treated your priests and the objects of your worship with as much respect? Who else would have conceded the privileges which you enjoy? for you hold rank in my councils, and both the police and the administration of my States are in your hands. I do not, however, seek to deny the evils with which I have afflicted you; but, alas! these evils have been the result of my enforced obedience to the cruel and perfidious orders of the Sublime Porte. It is to the Porte that these wrongs must be attributed, for if my actions be attentively regarded it will be seen that I only did harm when compelled thereto by the course of events. Interrogate my actions, they will speak more fully than a detailed apology.

"My position with regard to the Suliotes allowed no half-and-half measures. Having once broken with them, I was obliged either to drive them from my country or to exterminate them. I understood the political hatred of the Ottoman Cabinet too well not to know that it would declare war against me sooner or later, and I knew that resistance would be impossible, if on one side I had to repel the Ottoman aggression, and on the other to fight against the formidable Suliotes.

"I might say the same of the Parganiotes. You know that their town was the haunt of my enemies, and each time that I appealed to them to change their ways they answered only with insults and threats. They constantly aided the Suliotes with whom I was at war; and if at this moment they still were occupying Parga, you would see them throw open the gates of Epirus to the forces of the sultan. But all this does not prevent my being aware that my enemies blame me severely, and indeed I also blame myself, and deplore the faults which the difficulty of my position has entailed upon me. Strong in my repentance, I do not hesitate to address myself to those whom I have most grievously wounded. Thus I have long since recalled to my service a great number of Suliotes, and those who have responded to my invitation are occupying important posts near my person. To complete the reconciliation, I have written to those who are still in exile, desiring them to return fearlessly to their country, and I have certain information that this proposal has been everywhere accepted with enthusiasm. The Suliotes will soon return to their ancestral houses, and, reunited under my standard, will join me in combating the Osmanlis, our common enemies.

"As to the avarice of which I am accused, it seems easily justified by the constant necessity I was under of satisfying the inordinate cupidity of the Ottoman ministry, which incessantly made me pay dearly for tranquillity. This was a personal affair, I acknowledge, and so also is the accumulation of treasure made in order to support the war, which the Divan has at length declared."

Here Ali ceased, then having caused a barrel full of gold pieces to be emptied on the floor, he continued:

"Behold a part of the treasure I have preserved with so much care, and which has been specially obtained from the Turks, our common enemies: it is yours. I am now more than ever delighted at being the friend of the Greeks. Their bravery is a sure earnest of victory, and we will shortly re-establish the Greek Empire, and drive the Osmanlis across the Bosphorus. O bishops and priests of Issa the prophet! bless the arms of the Christians, your children. O primates! I call upon you to defend your rights, and to rule justly the brave nation associated with my interests."

This discourse produced very different impressions on the Christian priests and archons. Some replied only by raising looks of despair to Heaven, others murmured their adhesion. A great number remained uncertain, not knowing what to decide. The Mirdite chief, he who had refused to slaughter the Kardikiotes, declared that neither he nor any Skipetar of the Latin communion would bear arms against their legitimate sovereign the sultan. But his words were drowned by cries of "Long live Ali pacha! Long live the restorer of liberty!" uttered by some chiefs of adventurers and brigands.

IX

Yet next day, May 24th, 1820, Ali addressed a circular letter to his brothers the Christians, announcing that in future he would consider them as his most faithful subjects, and that henceforth he remitted the taxes paid to his own family. He wound up by asking for soldiers, but the Greeks having learnt the instability of his promises, remained deaf to his invitations. At the same time he sent messengers to the Montenegrins and the Servians, inciting them to revolt, and organised insurrections in Wallachia and Moldavia to the very environs of Constantinople.

Whilst the Ottoman vassals assembled only in small numbers and very slowly under their respective standards, every day there collected round the castle of Janina whole companies of Toxidae, of Tapazetae, and of Chamidae; so that Ali, knowing that Ismail Pacho Bey had boasted that he could arrive in sight of Janina without firing a gun, said in his turn that he would not treat with the Porte until he and his troops should be within eight leagues of Constantinople.

He had fortified and supplied with munitions of war Ochrida, Avlone, Cannia, Berat, Cleisoura, Premiti, the port of Panormus, Santi-Quaranta, Buthrotum, Delvino, Argyro-Castron, Tepelen, Parga, Prevesa, Sderli, Paramythia, Arta, the post of the Five Wells, Janina and its castles. These places contained four hundred and twenty cannons of all sizes, for the most part in bronze, mounted on siege-carriages, and seventy mortars. Besides these, there were in the castle by the lake, independently of the guns in position, forty field-pieces, sixty mountain guns, a number of Congreve rockets, formerly given him by the English, and an enormous quantity of munitions of war. Finally, he endeavoured to establish a line of semaphores between Janina and Prevesa, in order to have prompt news of the Turkish fleet, which was expected to appear on this coast.

Ali, whose strength seemed to increase with age, saw to everything and appeared everywhere; sometimes in a litter borne by his Albanians, sometimes in a carriage raised into a kind of platform, but it was more frequently on horseback that he appeared among his labourers. Often he sat on the bastions in the midst of the batteries, and conversed familiarly with those who surrounded him. He narrated the successes formerly obtained against the sultan by Kara Bazaklia, Vizier of Scodra, who, like himself, had been attained with the sentence of deprivation and excommunication; recounting how the rebel pacha, shut up in his citadel with seventy-two warriors, had seen collapse at his feet the united forces of four great provinces of the Ottoman Empire, commanded by twenty-two pachas, who were almost entirely annihilated in one day by the Guegues. He reminded them also, of the brilliant victory gained by Passevend Oglon, Pacha of Widdin, of quite recent memory, which is celebrated in the warlike songs of the Klephts of Roumelia.

Almost simultaneously, Ali's sons, Mouktar and Veli, arrived at Janina. Veli had been obliged, or thought himself obliged, to evacuate Lepanto by superior forces, and brought only discouraging news, especially as to the wavering fidelity of the Turks. Mouktar, on the contrary, who had just made a tour of inspection in the Musache, had only noticed favourable dispositions, and deluded himself with the idea that the Chaonians, who had taken up arms, had done so in order to aid his father. He was curiously mistaken, for these tribes hated Ali with a hatred all the deeper for being compelled to conceal it, and were only in arms in order to repel aggression.

The advice given by the sons to their father as to the manner of treating the Mohammedans differed widely in accordance with their respective opinions. Consequently a violent quarrel arose between them, ostensibly on account of this dispute, but in reality on the subject of their father's inheritance, which both equally coveted. Ali had brought all his treasure to Janina, and thenceforth neither son would leave the neighbourhood of so excellent a father. They overwhelmed him with marks of affection, and vowed that the one had left Lepanto, and the other Berat, only in order to share his danger. Ali was by no means duped by these protestations, of which he divined the motive only too well, and though he had never loved his sons, he suffered cruelly in discovering that he was not beloved by them.

Soon he had other troubles to endure. One of his gunners assassinated a servant of Veli's, and Ali ordered the murderer to be punished, but when the sentence was to be carried out the whole corps of artillery mutinied. In order to save appearances, the pacha was compelled to allow them to ask for the pardon of the criminal whom he dared not punish. This incident showed him that his authority was no longer paramount, and he began to doubt the fidelity of his soldiers. The arrival of the Ottoman fleet further enlightened him to his true position. Mussulman and Christian alike, all the inhabitants of Northern Albania, who had hitherto concealed their disaffection under an exaggerated semblance of devotion, now hastened to make their submission to the sultan. The Turks, continuing their success, laid siege to Parga, which was held by Mehemet, Veli's eldest son. He was prepared to make a good defence, but was betrayed by his troops, who opened the gates of the town, and he was compelled to surrender at discretion. He was handed over to the commander of the naval forces, by whom he was well treated, being assigned the best cabin in the admiral's ship and given a brilliant suite. He was assured that the sultan, whose only quarrel was with his grandfather, would show him favour, and would even deal mercifully with Ali, who, with his treasures, would merely be sent to an important province in Asia Minor. He was induced to write in this strain to his family and friends in order to induce them to lay down their arms.

The fall of Parga made a great impression on the Epirotes, who valued its possession far above its real importance. Ali rent his garments and cursed the days of his former good fortune, during which he had neither known how to moderate his resentment nor to foresee the possibility of any change of fortune.

The fall of Parga was succeeded by that of Arta of Mongliana, where was situated Ali's country house, and of the post of the Five Wells. Then came a yet more overwhelming piece of news: Omar Brionis, whom Ali, having formerly despoiled of its wealth, had none the less recently appointed general-in-chief, had gone over to the enemy with all his troops!

Ali then decided on carrying out a project he had formed in case of necessity, namely, on destroying the town of Janina, which would afford shelter to the enemy and a point of attack against the fortresses in which he was entrenched. When this resolution was known, the inhabitants thought only of saving themselves and their property from the ruin from which nothing could save their country. But most of them were only preparing to depart, when Ali gave leave to the Albanian soldiers yet faithful to him to sack the town.

The place was immediately invaded by an unbridled soldiery. The Metropolitan church, where Greeks and Turks alike deposited their gold, jewels, and merchandise, even as did the Greeks of old in the temples of the gods, became the first object of pillage. Nothing was respected. The cupboards containing sacred vestments were broken open; so were the tombs of the archbishops, in which were interred reliquaries adorned with precious stones; and the altar itself was defiled with the blood of ruffians who fought for chalices and silver crosses.

The town presented an equally terrible spectacle; neither Christians nor Mussulmans were spared, and the women's apartments, forcibly entered, were given up to violence. Some of the more courageous citizens endeavoured to defend their houses and families against these bandits, and the clash of arms mingled with cries and groans. All at once the roar of a terrible explosion rose above the other sounds, and a hail of bombs, shells, grenades, and rockets carried devastation and fire into the different quarters of the town, which soon presented the spectacle of an immense conflagration. Ali, seated on the great platform of the castle by the lake, which seemed to vomit fire like a volcano, directed the bombardment, pointing out the places which must be burnt. Churches, mosques, libraries, bazaars, houses, all were destroyed, and the only thing spared by the flames was the gallows, which remained standing in the midst of the ruins.

Of the thirty thousand persons who inhabited Janina a few hours previously, perhaps one half had escaped. But these had not fled many leagues before they encountered the outposts of the Ottoman army, which, instead of helping or protecting them, fell upon them, plundered them, and drove them towards the camp, where slavery awaited them. The unhappy fugitives, taken thus between fire and sword, death behind and slavery before, uttered a terrible cry, and fled in all directions. Those who escaped the Turks were stopped in the hill passes by the mountaineers rushing down to the rey; only large numbers who held together could force a passage.

In some cases terror bestows extraordinary strength; there were mothers who, with infants at the breast, covered on foot in one day the fourteen leagues which separate Janina from Arta. But others, seized with the pangs of travail in the midst of their flight, expired in the woods, after giving birth to babes, who, destitute of succour, did not survive their mothers. And young girls, having disfigured themselves by gashes, hid themselves in caves, where they died of terror and hunger.

The Albanians, intoxicated with plunder and debauchery, refused to return to the castle, and only thought of regaining their country and enjoying the fruit of their rapine. But they were assailed on the way by peasants covetous of their booty, and by those of Janina who had sought refuge with them. The roads and passes were strewn with corpses, and the trees by the roadside converted into gibbets. The murderers did not long survive their victims.

The ruins of Janina were still smoking when, on the 19th August, Pacho Bey made his entry. Having pitched his tent out of range of Ali's cannon, he proclaimed aloud the firman which inaugurated him as Pacha of Janina and Delvino, and then raised the tails, emblem of his dignity. Ali heard on the summit of his keep the acclamations of the Turks who saluted Pacho Bey, his former servant with the titles of Vali of Epirus, and Ghazi of Victorius. After this ceremony, the cadi read the sentence, confirmed by the Mufti, which declared Tepeleni Veli-Zade to have forfeited his dignities and to be excommunicated, adding an injunction to all the faithful that henceforth his name was not to be pronounced except with the addition of "Kara," or "black," which is bestowed on those cut off from the congregation of Sunnites, or Orthodox Mohammedans. A Marabout then cast a stone towards the castle, and the anathema upon "Kara Ali" was repeated by the whole Turkish army, ending with the cry of "Long live the sultan! So be it!"

But it was not by ecclesiastical thunders that three fortresses could be reduced, which were defended by artillerymen drawn from different European armies, who had established an excellent school for gunners and bombardiers. The besieged, having replied with hootings of contempt to the acclamations of the besiegers, proceeded to enforce their scorn with well-aimed cannon shots, while the rebel flotilla, dressed as if for a fete-day, passed slowly before the Turks, saluting them with cannon-shot if they ventured near the edge of the lake.

This noisy rhodomontade did not prevent Ali from being consumed with grief and anxiety. The sight of his own troops, now in the camp of Pacho Bey, the fear of being for ever separated from his sons, the thought of his grandson in the enemy's hands, all threw him into the deepest melancholy, and his sleepless eyes were constantly drowned in tears. He refused his food, and sat for seven days with untrimmed beard, clad in mourning, on a mat at the door of his antechamber, extending his hands to his soldiers, and imploring them to slay him rather than abandon him. His wives, seeing him in this state, and concluding all was lost, filled the air with their lamentations. All began to think that grief would bring Ali to the grave; but his soldiers, to whose protestations he at first refused any credit, represented to him that their fate was indissolubly linked with his. Pacho Bey having proclaimed that all taken in arms for Ali would be shot as sharers in rebellion, it was therefore their interest to support his resistance with all their power. They also pointed out that the campaign was already advanced, and that the Turkish army, which had forgotten its siege artillery at Constantinople, could not possibly procure any before the end of October, by which time the rains would begin, and the enemy would probably be short of food. Moreover, in any case, it being impossible to winter in a ruined town, the foe would be driven to seek shelter at a distance.

These representations, made with warm conviction, and supported by evidence, began to soothe the restless fever which was wasting Ali, and the gentle caresses and persuasions of Basillisa, the beautiful Christian captive, who had now been his wife for some time, completed the cure.

At the same time his sister Chainitza gave him an astonishing example of courage. She had persisted, in spite of all that could be said, in residing in her castle of Libokovo. The population, whom she had cruelly oppressed, demanded her death, but no one dared attack her. Superstition declared that the spirit of her mother, with whom she kept up a mysterious communication even beyond the portals of the grave, watched over her safety. The menacing form of Kamco had, it was said, appeared to several inhabitants of Tepelen, brandishing bones of the wretched Kardikiotes, and demanding fresh victims with loud cries. The desire of vengeance had urged some to brave these unknown dangers, and twice, a warrior, clothed in black, had warned them back, forbidding them to lay hands on a sacrilegious woman; whose punishment Heaven reserved to itself, and twice they had returned upon their footsteps.

But soon, ashamed of their terror, they attempted another attack, and came attired in the colour of the Prophet. This time no mysterious stranger appeared to forbid their passage, and with a cry they climbed the mountain listening for any supernatural warning. Nothing disturbed the silence and solitude save the bleating of flocks and the cries of birds of prey. Arrived on the platform of Libokovo, they prepared in silence to surprise the guards, believing the castle full of them. They approached crawling, like hunters who stalk a deer. Already they had reached the gate of the enclosure, and prepared to burst it open, when lo! it opened of itself, and they beheld Chainitza standing before them, a carabine in her hand, pistols in her belt, and, for all guard, two large dogs.

"Halt! ye daring ones," she cried; "neither my life nor my treasure will ever be at your mercy. Let one of you move a step without my permission, and this place and the ground beneath your feet will engulf you. Ten thousand pounds of powder are in these cellars. I will, however, grant your pardon, unworthy though you are. I will even allow you to take these sacks filled with gold; they may recompense you for the losses which my brother's enemies have recently inflicted on you. But depart this instant without a word, and dare not to trouble me again; I have other means of destruction at command besides gunpowder. Life is nothing to me, remember that; but your mountains may yet at my command become the tomb of your wives and children. Go!"

She ceased, and her would-be murderers fled in terror.

Shortly after the plague broke out in these mountains, Chainitza had distributed infected garments among gipsies, who scattered contagion wherever they went.

"We are indeed of the same blood!" cried Ali with pride, when he heard of his sister's conduct; and from that hour he appeared to regain all the fire and audacity of his youth. When, a few days later, he was informed that Mouktar and Veli, seduced by the brilliant promises of Pacha Bey, had surrendered Prevesa and Argyro-Castron, "It does not surprise me," he observed coldly. "I have long known them to be unworthy of being my sons, and henceforth my only children and heirs are those who defend my cause." And on hearing a report that both had been beheaded by Pacha Bey's order, he contented himself with saying, "They betrayed their father, and have only received their deserts; speak no more of them." And to show how little it discouraged him, he redoubled his fire upon the Turks.

But the latter, who had at length obtained some artillery, answered his fire with vigour, and began to rally to discrown the old pacha's fortress. Feeling that the danger was pressing, Ali redoubled both his prudence and activity. His immense treasures were the real reason of the war waged against him, and these might induce his own soldiers to rebel, in order to become masters of them. He resolved to protect them from either surprise or conquest. The sum necessary for present use was deposited in the powder magazine, so that, if driven to extremity, it might be destroyed in a moment; the remainder was enclosed in strong-boxes, and sunk in different parts of the lake. This labour lasted a fortnight, when, finally, Ali put to death the gipsies who had been employed about it, in order that the secret might remain with himself.

While he thus set his own affairs in order, he applied himself to the troubling those of his adversary. A great number of Suliots had joined the Ottoman army in order to assist in the destruction of him who formerly had ruined their country. Their camp, which for a long time had enjoyed immunity from the guns of Janina, was one day overwhelmed with bombs. The Suliots were terrified, until they remarked that the bombs did not burst. They then, much astonished, proceeded to pick up and examine these projectiles. Instead of a match, they found rolls of paper enclosed in a wooden cylinder, on which was engraved these words, "Open carefully." The paper contained a truly Macchiavellian letter from Ali, which began by saying that they were quite justified in having taken up arms against him, and added that he now sent them a part of the pay of which the traitorous Ismail was defrauding them, and that the bombs thrown into their cantonment contained six thousand sequins in gold. He begged them to amuse Ismail by complaints and recriminations, while his gondola should by night fetch one of them, to whom he would communicate what more he had to say. If they accepted his proposition, they were to light three fires as a signal.

The signal was not long in appearing. Ali despatched his barge, which took on board a monk, the spiritual chief of the Suliots. He was clothed in sackcloth, and repeated the prayers for the dying, as one going to execution. Ali, however, received him with the utmost cordiality: He assured the priest of his repentance, his good intentions, his esteem for the Greek captains, and then gave him a paper which startled him considerably. It was a despatch, intercepted by Ali, from Khalid Effendi to the Seraskier Ismail, ordering the latter to exterminate all Christians capable of bearing arms. All male children were to be circumcised, and brought up to form a legion drilled in European fashion; and the letter went on to explain how the Suliots, the Armatolis, the Greek races of the mainland and those of the Archipelago should be disposed of. Seeing the effect produced on the monk by the perusal of this paper, Ali hastened to make him the most advantageous offers, declaring that his own wish was to give Greece a political existence, and only requiring that the Suliot captains should send him a certain number of their children as hostages. He then had cloaks and arms brought which he presented to the monk, dismissing him in haste, in order that darkness might favour his return.

The next day Ali was resting, with his head on Basilissa's lap, when he was informed that the enemy was advancing upon the intrenchments which had been raised in the midst of the ruins of Janina. Already the outposts had been forced, and the fury of the assailants threatened to triumph over all obstacles. Ali immediately ordered a sortie of all his troops, announcing that he himself would conduct it. His master of the horse brought him the famous Arab charger called the Dervish, his chief huntsman presented him with his guns, weapons still famous in Epirus, where they figure in the ballads of the Skipetars. The first was an enormous gun, of Versailles manufacture, formerly presented by the conqueror of the Pyramids to Djezzar, the Pacha of St. Jean-d'Arc, who amused himself by enclosing living victims in the walls of his palace, in order that he might hear their groans in the midst of his festivities. Next came a carabine given to the Pacha of Janina in the name of Napoleon in 1806; then the battle musket of Charles XII of Sweden, and finally – the much revered sabre of Krim-Guerai. The signal was given; the draw bridge crossed; the Guegues and other adventurers uttered a terrific shout; to which the cries of the assailants replied. Ali placed himself on a height, whence his eagle eye sought to discern the hostile chiefs; but he called and defied Pacho Bey in vain. Perceiving Hassan-Stamboul, colonel of the Imperial bombardiers outside his battery, Ali demanded the gun of Djezzar, and laid him dead on the spot. He then took the carabine of Napoleon, and shot with it Kekriman, Bey of Sponga, whom he had formerly appointed Pacha of Lepanto. The enemy now became aware of his presence, and sent a lively fusillade in his direction; but the balls seemed to diverge from his person. As soon as the smoke cleared, he perceived Capelan, Pacha of Croie, who had been his guest, and wounded him mortally in the chest. Capelan uttered a sharp cry, and his terrified horse caused disorder in the ranks. Ali picked off a large number of officers, one after another; every shot was mortal, and his enemies began to regard him in the light of a destroying angel. Disorder spread through the forces of the Seraskier, who retreated hastily to his intrenchments.

The Suliots meanwhile sent a deputation to Ismail offering their submission, and seeking to regain their country in a peaceful manner; but, being received by him with the most humiliating contempt, they resolved to make common cause with Ali. They hesitated over the demand for hostages, and at length required Ali's grandson, Hussien Pacha, in exchange. After many difficulties, Ali at length consented, and the agreement was concluded. The Suliots received five hundred thousand piastres and a hundred and fifty charges of ammunition; Hussien Pacha was given up to them, and they left the Ottoman camp at dead of night. Morco Botzaris remained with three hundred and twenty men, threw down the palisades, and then ascending Mount Paktoras with his troops, waited for dawn in order to announce his defection to the Turkish army. As soon as the sun appeared he ordered a general salvo of artillery and shouted his war-cry. A few Turks in charge of an outpost were slain, the rest fled. A cry of "To arms" was raised, and the standard of the Cross floated before the camp of the infidels.

Signs and omens of a coming general insurrection appeared on all sides; there was no lack of prodigies, visions, or popular rumours, and the Mohammedans became possessed with the idea that the last hour of their rule in Greece had struck. Ali Pacha favoured the general demoralisation; and his agents, scattered throughout the land, fanned the flame of revolt. Ismail Pacha was deprived of his title of Seraskier, and superseded by Kursheed Pacha. As soon as Ali heard this, he sent a messenger to Kursheed, hoping to influence him in his favour. Ismail, distrusting the Skipetars, who formed part of his troops, demanded hostages from them. The Skipetars were indignant, and Ali, hearing of their discontent, wrote inviting them to return to him, and endeavouring to dazzle them by the most brilliant promises. These overtures were received by the offended troops with enthusiasm, and Alexis Noutza, Ali's former general, who had forsaken him for Ismail, but who had secretly returned to his allegiance and acted as a spy on the Imperial army, was deputed to treat with him. As soon as he arrived, Ali began to enact a comedy in the intention of rebutting the accusation of incest with his daughter-in-law Zobeide; for this charge, which, since Veli himself had revealed the secret of their common shame, could only be met by vague denials, had never ceased to produce a most unfavourable impression on Noutza's mind. Scarcely had he entered the castle by the lake, when Ali rushed to meet him, and flung himself into his arms. In presence of his officers and the garrison, he loaded him with the most tender names, calling him his son, his beloved Alexis, his own legitimate child, even as Salik Pacha. He burst into tears, and, with terrible oaths, called Heaven to witness that Mouktar and Veli, whom he disavowed on account of their cowardice, were the adulterous offspring of Emineh's amours. Then, raising his hand against the tomb of her whom he had loved so much, he drew the stupefied Noutza into the recess of a casemate, and sending for Basilissa, presented him to her as a beloved son, whom only political considerations had compelled him to keep at a distance, because, being born of a Christian mother, he had been brought up in the faith of Jesus.

Having thus softened the suspicions of his soldiers, Ali resumed his underground intrigues. The Suliots had informed him that the sultan had made them extremely advantageous offers if they would return to his service, and they demanded pressingly that Ali should give up to them the citadel of Kiapha, which was still in his possession, and which commanded Suli. He replied with the information that he intended, January 26, to attack the camp of Pacho Bey early in the morning, and requested their assistance. In order to cause a diversion, they were to descend into the valley of Janina at night, and occupy a position which he pointed out to them, and he gave them the word "flouri" as password for the night. If successful, he undertook to grant their request.

Ali's letter was intercepted, and fell into Ismail's hands, who immediately conceived a plan for snaring his enemy in his own toils. When the night fixed by Ali arrived, the Seraskier marched out a strong division under the command of Omar Brionis, who had been recently appointed Pacha, and who was instructed to proceed along the western slope of Mount Paktoras as far as the village of Besdoune, where he was to place an outpost, and then to retire along the other side of the mountain, so that, being visible in the starlight, the sentinels placed to watch on the hostile towers might take his men for the Suliots and report to Ali that the position of Saint-Nicolas, assigned to them, had been occupied as arranged. All preparations for battle were made, and the two mortal enemies, Ismail and Ali, retired to rest, each cherishing the darling hope of shortly annihilating his rival.

At break of day a lively cannonade, proceeding from the castle of the lake and from Lithoritza, announced that the besieged intended a sortie. Soon Ali's Skipetars, preceded by a detachment of French, Italians, and Swiss, rushed through the Ottoman fire and carried the first redoubt, held by Ibrahim-Aga-Stamboul. They found six pieces of cannon, which the Turks, notwithstanding their terror, had had time to spike. This misadventure, for they had hoped to turn the artillery against the intrenched camp, decided Ali's men on attacking the second redoubt, commanded by the chief bombardier. The Asiatic troops of Baltadgi Pacha rushed to its defence. At their head appeared the chief Imaun of the army, mounted on a richly caparisoned mule and repeating the curse fulminated by the mufti against Ali, his adherents, his castles, and even his cannons, which it was supposed might be rendered harmless by these adjurations. Ali's Mohammedan Skipetars averted their eyes, and spat into their bosoms, hoping thus to escape the evil influence. A superstitious terror was beginning to spread among them, when a French adventurer took aim at the Imaun and brought him down, amid the acclamations of the soldiers; whereupon the Asiatics, imagining that Eblis himself fought against them, retired within the intrenchments, whither the Skipetars, no longer fearing the curse, pursued them vigorously.

At the same time, however, a very different action was proceeding at the northern end of the besiegers' intrenchments. Ali left his castle of the lake, preceded by twelve torch-bearers carrying braziers filled with lighted pitch-wood, and advanced towards the shore of Saint-Nicolas, expecting to unite with the Suliots. He stopped in the middle of the ruins to wait for sunrise, and while there heard that his troops had carried the battery of Ibrahim-Aga-Stamboul. Overjoyed, he ordered them to press on to the second intrenchment, promising that in an hour, when he should have been joined by the Suliots, he would support them, and he then pushed forward, preceded by two field-pieces with their waggons, and followed by fifteen hundred men, as far as a large plateau on which he perceived at a little distance an encampment which he supposed to be that of the Suliots. He then ordered the Mirdite prince, Kyr Lekos, to advance with an escort of twenty-five men, and when within hearing distance to wave a blue flag and call out the password. An Imperial officer replied with the countersign "flouri," and Lekos immediately sent back word to Ali to advance. His orderly hastened back, and the prince entered the camp, where he and his escort were immediately surrounded and slain.

On receiving the message, Ali began to advance, but cautiously, being uneasy at seeing no signs of the Mirdite troop. Suddenly, furious cries, and a lively fusillade, proceeding from the vineyards and thickets, announced that he had fallen into a trap, and at the same moment Omar Pacha fell upon his advance guard, which broke, crying "Treason!"

Ali sabred the fugitives mercilessly, but fear carried them away, and, forced to follow the crowd, he perceived the Kersales and Baltadgi Pacha descending the side of Mount Paktoras, intending to cut off his retreat. He attempted another route, hastening towards the road to Dgeleva, but found it held by the Tapagetae under the Bimbashi Aslon of Argyro-Castron. He was surrounded; all seemed lost, and feeling that his last hour had come, he thought only of selling his life as dearly as possible. Collecting his bravest soldiers round him, he prepared for a last rush on Omar Pacha, when, suddenly, with an inspiration born of despair, he ordered his ammunition waggons to be blown up. The Kersales, who were about to seize them, vanished in the explosion, which scattered a hail of stones and debris far and wide. Under cover of the smoke and general confusion, Ali succeeded in withdrawing his men to the shelter of the guns of his castle of Litharitza, where he continued the fight in order to give time to the fugitives to rally, and to give the support he had promised to those fighting on the other slope; who, in the meantime, had carried the second battery and were attacking the fortified camp. Here the Seraskier Ismail met them with a resistance so well managed, that he was able to conceal the attack he was preparing to make on their rear. Ali, guessing that the object of Ismail's manoeuvres was to crush those whom he had promised to help, and unable, on account of the distance, either to support or to warn them, endeavoured to impede Omar pacha, hoping still that his Skipetars might either see or hear him. He encouraged the fugitives, who recognised him from afar by his scarlet dolman, by the dazzling whiteness of his horse, and by the terrible cries which he uttered; for, in the heat of battle, this extraordinary man appeared to have regained the vigour and audacity of his youth. Twenty times he led his soldiers to the charge, and as often was forced to recoil towards his castles. He brought up his reserves, but in vain. Fate had declared against him. His troops which were attacking the intrenched camp found themselves taken between two fires, and he could not help them. Foaming with passion, he threatened to rush singly into the midst of his enemies. His officers besought him to calm himself, and, receiving only refusals, at last threatened to lay hands upon him if he persisted in exposing himself like a private soldier. Subdued by this unaccustomed opposition, Ali allowed himself to be forced back into the castle by the lake, while his soldiers dispersed in various directions.

But even this defeat did not discourage the fierce pacha. Reduced to extremity, he yet entertained the hope of shaking the Ottoman Empire, and from the recesses of his fortress he agitated the whole of Greece. The insurrection which he had stirred up, without foreseeing what the results might be, was spreading with the rapidity of a lighted train of powder, and the Mohammedans were beginning to tremble, when at length Kursheed pacha, having crossed the Pindus at the head of an army of eighty thousand men, arrived before Janina.

His tent had hardly been pitched, when Ali caused a salute of twenty-one guns to be fired in his honour, and sent a messenger, bearing a letter of congratulation on his safe arrival. This letter, artful and insinuating, was calculated to make a deep impression on Kursheed. Ali wrote that, being driven by the infamous lies of a former servant, called Pacho Bey, into resisting, not indeed the authority of the sultan, before whom he humbly bent his head weighed down with years and grief, but the perfidious plots of His Highness's advisers, he considered himself happy in his misfortunes to have dealings with a vizier noted for his lofty qualities. He then added that these rare merits had doubtless been very far from being estimated at their proper value by a Divan in which men were only classed in accordance with the sums they laid out in gratifying the rapacity of the ministers. Otherwise, how came it about that Kursheed pacha, Viceroy of Egypt – after the departure of the French, the conqueror of the Mamelukes, was only rewarded for these services by being recalled without a reason? Having been twice Romili-Valicy, why, when he should have enjoyed the reward of his labours, was he relegated to the obscure post of Salonica? And, when appointed Grand Vizier and sent to pacify Servia, instead of being entrusted with the government of this kingdom which he had reconquered for the sultan, why was he hastily despatched to Aleppo to repress a trifling sedition of emirs and janissaries? Now, scarcely arrived in the Morea, his powerful arm was to be employed against an aged man.

Ali then plunged into details, related the pillaging, avarice, and imperious dealing of Pacho Bey, as well as of the pachas subordinate to him; how they had alienated the public mind, how they had succeeded in offending the Armatolis, and especially the Suliots, who might be brought back to their duty with less trouble than these imprudent chiefs had taken to estrange them. He gave a mass of special information on this subject, and explained that in advising the Suliots to retire to their mountains he had really only put them in a false position as long as he retained possession of the fort of Kiapha, which is the key of the Selleide.

The Seraskier replied in a friendly manner, ordered the military salute to be returned in Ali's honour, shot for shot, and forbade that henceforth a person of the valour and intrepidity of the Lion of Tepelen should be described by the epithet of "excommunicated." He also spoke of him by his title of "vizier," which he declared he had never forfeited the right to use; and he also stated that he had only entered Epirus as a peace-maker. Kursheed's emissaries had just seized some letters sent by Prince Alexander Ypsilanti to the Greek captains at Epirus. Without going into details of the events which led to the Greek insurrection, the prince advised the Polemarchs, chiefs of the Selleid, to aid Ali Pacha in his revolt against the Porte, but to so arrange matters that they could easily detach themselves again, their only aim being to seize his treasures, which might be used to procure the freedom of Greece.

These letters a messenger from Kursheed delivered to Ali. They produced such an impression upon his mind that he secretly resolved only to make use of the Greeks, and to sacrifice them to his own designs, if he could not inflict a terrible vengeance on their perfidy. He heard from the messenger at the same time of the agitation in European Turkey, the hopes of the Christians, and the apprehension of a rupture between the Porte and Russia. It was necessary to lay aside vain resentment and to unite against these threatening dangers. Kursheed Pacha was, said his messenger, ready to consider favourably any propositions likely to lead to a prompt pacification, and would value such a result far more highly than the glory of subduing by means of the imposing force at his command, a valiant prince whom he had always regarded as one of the strongest bulwarks of the Ottoman Empire. This information produced a different effect upon Ali to that intended by the Seraskier. Passing suddenly from the depth of despondency to the height of pride, he imagined that these overtures of reconciliation were only a proof of the inability of his foes to subdue him, and he sent the following propositions to Kursheed Pacha:

"If the first duty of a prince is to do justice, that of his subjects is to remain faithful, and obey him in all things. From this principle we derive that of rewards and punishments, and although my services might sufficiently justify my conduct to all time, I nevertheless acknowledge that I have deserved the wrath of the sultan, since he has raised the arm of his anger against the head of his slave. Having humbly implored his pardon, I fear not to invoke his severity towards those who have abused his confidence. With this object I offer – First, to pay the expenses of the war and the tribute in arrears due from my Government without delay. Secondly, as it is important for the sake of example that the treason of an inferior towards his superior should receive fitting chastisement, I demand that Pacho Bey, formerly in my service, should be beheaded, he being the real rebel, and the cause of the public calamities which are afflicting the faithful of Islam. Thirdly, I require that for the rest of my life I shall retain, without annual re-investiture, my pachalik of Janina, the coast of Epirus, Acarnania and its dependencies, subject to the rights, charges and tribute due now and hereafter to the sultan. Fourthly, I demand amnesty and oblivion of the past for all those who have served me until now. And if these conditions are not accepted without modifications, I am prepared to defend myself to the last.

"Given at the castle of Janina, March 7, 1821."

X

This mixture of arrogance and submission only merited indignation, but it suited Kursheed to dissemble. He replied that, assenting to such propositions being beyond his powers, he would transmit them to Constantinople, and that hostilities might be suspended, if Ali wished, until the courier could return.

Being quite as cunning as Ali himself, Kursheed profited by the truce to carry on intrigues against him. He corrupted one of the chiefs of the garrison, Metzo-Abbas by name, who obtained pardon for himself and fifty followers, with permission to return to their homes. But this clemency appeared to have seduced also four hundred Skipetars who made use of the amnesty and the money with which Ali provided them, to raise Toxis and the Tapygetae in the latter's favour. Thus the Seraskier's scheme turned against himself, and he perceived he had been deceived by Ali's seeming apathy, which certainly did not mean dread of defection. In fact, no man worth anything could have abandoned him, supported as he seemed to be by almost supernatural courage. Suffering from a violent attack of gout, a malady he had never before experienced, the pacha, at the age of eighty-one, was daily carried to the most exposed place on the ramparts of his castle. There, facing the hostile batteries, he gave audience to whoever wished to see him. On this exposed platform he held his councils, despatched orders, and indicated to what points his guns should be directed. Illumined by the flashes of fire, his figure assumed fantastic and weird shapes. The balls sung in the air, the bullets hailed around him, the noise drew blood from the ears of those with him. Calm and immovable, he gave signals to the soldiers who were still occupying part of the ruins of Janina, and encouraged them by voice and gesture. Observing the enemy's movements by the help of a telescope, he improvised means of counteracting them. Sometimes he amused himself by greeting curious persons and new-comers after a fashion of his own. Thus the chancellor of the French Consul at Prevesa, sent as an envoy to Kursheed Pacha, had scarcely entered the lodging assigned to him, when he was visited by a bomb which caused him to leave it again with all haste. This greeting was due to Ali's chief engineer, Caretto, who next day sent a whole shower of balls and shells into the midst of a group of Frenchmen, whose curiosity had brought them to Tika, where Kursheed was forming a battery. "It is time," said Ali, "that these contemptible gossip-mongers should find listening at doors may become uncomfortable. I have furnished matter enough for them to talk about. Frangistan (Christendom) shall henceforth hear only of my triumph or my fall, which will leave it considerable trouble to pacify." Then, after a moment's silence, he ordered the public criers to inform his soldiers of the insurrections in Wallachia and the Morea, which news, proclaimed from the ramparts, and spreading immediately in the Imperial camp, caused there much dejection.

The Greeks were now everywhere proclaiming their independence, and Kursheed found himself unexpectedly surrounded by enemies. His position threatened to become worse if the siege of Janina dragged on much longer. He seized the island in the middle of the lake, and threw up redoubts upon it, whence he kept up an incessant fire on the southern front of the castle of Litharitza, and, a practicable trench of nearly forty feet having been made, an assault was decided on. The troops marched out boldly, and performed prodigies of valour; but at the end of an hour, Ali, carried on a litter because of his gout, having led a sortie, the besiegers were compelled to give way and retire to their intrenchments, leaving three hundred dead at the foot of the rampart. "The Pindian bear is yet alive," said Ali in a message to Kursheed; "thou mayest take thy dead and bury them; I give them up without ransom, and as I shall always do when thou attackest me as a brave man ought." Then, having entered his fortress amid the acclamations of his soldiers, he remarked on hearing of the general rising of Greece and the Archipelago, "It is enough! two men have ruined Turkey!" He then remained silent, and vouchsafed no explanation of this prophetic sentence.

Ali did not on this occasion manifest his usual delight on having gained a success. As soon as he was alone with Basilissa, he informed her with tears of the death of Chainitza. A sudden apoplexy had stricken this beloved sister, the life of his councils, in her palace of Libokovo, where she remained undisturbed until her death. She owed this special favour to her riches and to the intercession of her nephew, Djiladin Pacha of Ochcrida, who was reserved by fate to perform the funeral obsequies of the guilty race of Tepelen.

A few months afterwards, Ibrahim Pacha of Berat died of poison, being the last victim whom Chainitza had demanded from her brother.

Ali's position was becoming daily more difficult, when the time of Ramadan arrived, during which the Turks relax hostilities, and a species of truce ensued. Ali himself appeared to respect the old popular customs, and allowed his Mohammedan soldiers to visit the enemy's outposts and confer on the subject of various religious ceremonies. Discipline was relaxed in Kursheed's camp, and Ali profited thereby to ascertain the smallest details of all that passed.

He learned from his spies that the general's staff, counting on the "Truce of God," a tacit suspension of all hostilities during the feast of Bairam, the Mohammedan Easter, intended to repair to the chief mosque, in the quarter of Loutcha. This building, spared by the bombs, had until now been respected by both sides. Ali, according to reports spread by himself, was supposed to be ill, weakened by fasting, and terrified into a renewal of devotion, and not likely to give trouble on so sacred a day. Nevertheless he ordered Caretto to turn thirty guns against the mosque, cannon, mortars and howitzers, intending, he said, to solemnise Bairam by discharges of artillery. As soon as he was sure that the whole of the staff had entered the mosque, he gave the signal.

Instantly, from the assembled thirty pieces, there issued a storm of shells, grenades and cannon-balls. With a terrific noise, the mosque crumbled together, amid the cries of pain and rage of the crowd inside crushed in the ruins. At the end of a quarter of an hour the wind dispersed the smoke, and disclosed a burning crater, with the large cypresses which surrounded the building blazing as if they had been torches lighted for the funeral ceremonies of sixty captains and two hundred soldiers.

"Ali Pacha is yet alive!" cried the old Homeric hero of Janina, leaping with joy; and his words, passing from mouth to mouth, spread yet more terror amid Kursheed's soldiers, already overwhelmed by the horrible spectacle passing before their eyes.

Almost on the same day, Ali from the height of his keep beheld the standard of the Cross waving in the distance. The rebellious Greeks were bent on attacking Kursheed. The insurrection promoted by the Vizier of Janina had passed far beyond the point he intended, and the rising had become a revolution. The delight which Ali first evinced cooled rapidly before this consideration, and was extinguished in grief when he found that a conflagration, caused by the besiegers' fire, had consumed part of his store in the castle by the lake. Kursheed, thinking that this event must have shaken the old lion's resolution, recommenced negotiations, choosing the Kiaia of Moustai Pacha: as an envoy, who gave Ali a remarkable warning. "Reflect," said he, "that these rebels bear the sign of the Cross on their standards. You are now only an instrument in their hands. Beware lest you become the victim of their policy." Ali understood the danger, and had the sultan been better advised, he would have pardoned Ali on condition of again bringing Hellas under his iron yoke. It is possible that the Greeks might not have prevailed against an enemy so formidable and a brain so fertile in intrigue. But so simple an idea was far beyond the united intellect of the Divan, which never rose above idle display. As soon as these negotiations had commenced, Kursheed filled the roads with his couriers, sending often two in a day to Constantinople, from whence as many were sent to him. This state of things lasted more than three weeks, when it became known that Ali, who had made good use of his time in replacing the stores lost in the conflagration, buying actually from the Kiaia himself a part of the provisions brought by him for the Imperial camp, refused to accept the Ottoman ultimatum. Troubles which broke out at the moment of the rupture of the negotiations proved that he foresaw the probable result.

Kursheed was recompensed for the deception by which he had been duped by the reduction of the fortress of Litharitza. The Guegue Skipetars, who composed the garrison, badly paid, wearied out by the long siege, and won by the Seraskier's bribes, took advantage of the fact that the time of their engagement with Ali had elapsed some months previously, and, delivering up the fortress they defended, passed over to the enemy. Henceforth Ali's force consisted of only six hundred men.

It was to be feared that this handful of men might also become a prey to discouragement, and might surrender their chief to an enemy who had received all fugitives with kindness. The Greek insurgents dreaded such an event, which would have turned all Kursheed's army, hitherto detained before the castle, of Janina loose upon themselves. Therefore they hastened to send to their former enemy, now their ally, assistance which he declined to accept. Ali saw himself surrounded by enemies thirsting for his wealth, and his avarice increasing with the danger, he had for some months past refused to pay his defenders. He contented himself with informing his captains of the insurgents' offer, and telling them that he was confident that bravery such as theirs required no rein-forcement. And when some of them besought him to at least receive two or three hundred Palikars into the castle, "No," said he; "old serpents always remain old serpents: I distrust the Suliots and their friendship."

Ignorant of Ali's decision, the Greeks of the Selleid were advancing, as well as the Toxidae, towards Janina, when they received the following letter from Ali Pacha:

"My well-beloved children, I have just learned that you are preparing to despatch a party of your Palikars against our common enemy, Kursheed. I desire to inform you that this my fortress is impregnable, and that I can hold out against him for several years. The only service I require of your courage is that you should reduce Arta, and take alive Ismail Pacho Bey, my former servant, the mortal enemy of my family, and the author of the evils and frightful calamities which have so long oppressed our unhappy country, which he has laid waste before our eyes. Use your best efforts to accomplish this; it will strike at the root of the evil, and my treasures shall reward your Palikars, whose courage every day gains a higher value in my eyes."

Furious at this mystification, the Suliots retired to their mountains, and Kursheed profited by the discontent Ali's conduct had caused, to win over the Toxide Skipetars, with their commanders Tahir Abbas and Hagi Bessiaris, who only made two conditions: one, that Ismail Pacho Bey, their personal enemy, should be deposed; the other, that the life of their old vizier should be respected.

The first condition was faithfully adhered to by Kursheed, actuated by private motives different from those which he gave publicly, and Ismail Pacho Bey was solemnly deposed. The tails, emblems of his authority, were removed; he resigned the plumes of office; his soldiers forsook him, his servants followed suit. Fallen to the lowest rank, he was soon thrown into prison, where he only blamed Fate for his misfortunes. All the Skipetar Agas hastened to place themselves under Kursheed's standard, and enormous forces now threatened Janina. All Epirus awaited the denoument with anxiety.

Had he been less avaricious, Ali might have enlisted all the adventurers with whom the East was swarming, and made the sultan tremble in his capital. But the aged pacha clung passionately to his treasures. He feared also, perhaps not unreasonably, that those by whose aid he might triumph would some day become his master. He long deceived himself with the idea that the English, who had sold Parga to him, would never allow a Turkish fleet to enter the Ionian Sea. Mistaken on this point, his foresight was equally at fault with regard to the cowardice of his sons. The defection of his troops was not less fatal, and he only understood the bearing of the Greek insurrection which he himself had provoked, so far as to see that in this struggle he was merely an instrument in procuring the freedom of a country which he had too cruelly oppressed to be able to hold even an inferior rank in it. His last letter to the Suliots opened the eyes of his followers, but under the influence of a sort of polite modesty these were at least anxious to stipulate for the life of their vizier. Kursheed was obliged to produce firmans from the Porte, declaring that if Ali Tepelen submitted, the royal promise given to his sons should be kept, and that he should, with them, be transferred to Asia Minor, as also his harem, his servants; and his treasures, and allowed to finish his days in peace. Letters from Ali's sons were shown to the Agas, testifying to the good treatment they had experienced in their exile; and whether the latter believed all this, or whether they merely sought to satisfy their own consciences, they henceforth thought only of inducing their rebellious chief to submit. Finally, eight months' pay, given them in advance, proved decisive, and they frankly embraced the cause of the sultan.

The garrison of the castle on the lake, whom Ali seemed anxious to offend as much as possible, by refusing their pay, he thinking them so compromised that they would not venture even to accept an amnesty guaranteed by the mufti, began to desert as soon as they knew the Toxidae had arrived at the Imperial camp. Every night these Skipetars who could cross the moat betook themselves to Kursheed's quarters. One single man yet baffled all the efforts of the besiegers. The chief engineer, Caretto, like another Archimedes, still carried terror into the midst of their camp.

Although reduced to the direst misery, Caretto could not forget that he owed his life to the master who now only repaid his services with the most sordid ingratitude. When he had first come to Epirus, Ali, recognising his ability, became anxious to retain him, but without incurring any expense. He ascertained that the Neapolitan was passionately in love with a Mohammedan girl named Nekibi, who returned his affection. Acting under Ali's orders, Tahir Abbas accused the woman before the cadi of sacrilegious intercourse with an infidel. She could only escape death by the apostasy of her lover; if he refused to deny his God, he shared her fate, and both would perish at the stake. Caretto refused to renounce his religion, but only Nekibi suffered death. Caretto was withdrawn from execution, and Ali kept him concealed in a place of safety, whence he produced him in the time of need. No one had served him with greater zeal; it is even possible that a man of this type would have died at his post, had his cup not been filled with mortification and insult.

Eluding the vigilance of Athanasius Vaya, whose charge it was to keep guard over him, Caretto let himself down by a cord fastened to the end of a cannon: He fell at the foot of the rampart, and thence dragged himself, with a broken arm, to the opposite camp. He had become nearly blind through the explosion of a cartridge which had burnt his face. He was received as well as a Christian from whom there was now nothing to fear, could expect. He received the bread of charity, and as a refugee is only valued in proportion to the use which can be made of him, he was despised and forgotten.

The desertion of Caretto was soon followed by a defection which annihilated Ali's last hopes. The garrison which had given him so many proofs of devotion, discouraged by his avarice, suffering from a disastrous epidemic, and no longer equal to the necessary labour in defence of the place, opened all the gates simultaneously to the enemy. But the besiegers, fearing a trap, advanced very slowly; so that Ali, who had long prepared against every sort of surprise, had time to gain a place which he called his "refuge."

It was a sort of fortified enclosure, of solid masonry, bristling with cannon, which surrounded the private apartments of his seraglio, called the "Women's Tower." He had taken care to demolish everything which could be set on fire, reserving only a mosque and the tomb of his wife Emineh, whose phantom, after announcing an eternal repose, had ceased to haunt him. Beneath was an immense natural cave, in which he had stored ammunition, precious articles, provisions, and the treasures which had not been sunk in the lake. In this cave an apartment had been made for Basilissa and his harem, also a shelter in which he retired to sleep when exhausted with fatigue. This place was his last resort, a kind of mausoleum; and he did not seem distressed at beholding the castle in the hands of his enemies. He calmly allowed them to occupy the entrance, deliver their hostages, overrun the ramparts, count the cannon which were on the platforms, crumbling from the hostile shells; but when they came within hearing, he demanded by one of his servants that Kursheed should send him an envoy of distinction; meanwhile he forbade anyone to pass beyond a certain place which he pointed out.

Kursheed, imagining that, being in the last extremity, he would capitulate, sent out Tahir Abbas and Hagi Bessiaris. Ali listened without reproaching them for their treachery, but simply observed that he wished to meet some of the chief officers.

The Seraskier then deputed his keeper of the wardrobe, accompanied by his keeper of the seals and other persons of quality. Ali received them with all ceremony, and, after the usual compliments had been exchanged, invited them to descend with him into the cavern. There he showed them more than two thousand barrels of powder carefully arranged beneath his treasures, his remaining provisions, and a number of valuable objects which adorned this slumbering volcano. He showed them also his bedroom, a sort of cell richly furnished, and close to the powder. It could be reached only by means of three doors, the secret of which was known to no one but himself. Alongside of this was the harem, and in the neighbouring mosque was quartered his garrison, consisting of fifty men, all ready to bury themselves under the ruins of this fortification, the only spot remaining to him of all Greece, which had formerly bent beneath his authority.

After this exhibition, Ali presented one of his most devoted followers to the envoys. Selim, who watched over the fire, was a youth in appearance as gentle as his heart was intrepid, and his special duty was to be in readiness to blow up the whole place at any moment. The pacha gave him his hand to kiss, inquiring if he were ready to die, to which he only responded by pressing his master's hand fervently to his lips. He never took his eyes off Ali, and the lantern, near which a match was constantly smoking, was entrusted only to him and to Ali, who took turns with him in watching it. Ali drew a pistol from his belt, making as if to turn it towards the powder magazine, and the envoys fell at his feet, uttering involuntary cries of terror. He smiled at their fears, and assured them that, being wearied of the weight of his weapons, he had only intended to relieve himself of some of them. He then begged them to seat themselves, and added that he should like even a more terrible funeral than that which they had just ascribed to him. "I do not wish to drag down with me," he exclaimed, "those who have come to visit me as friends; it is Kursheed, whom I have long regarded as my brother, his chiefs, those who have betrayed me, his whole army in short, whom I desire to follow me to the tomb – a sacrifice which will be worthy of my renown, and of the brilliant end to which I aspire."

The envoys gazed at him with stupefaction, which did not diminish when Ali further informed them that they were not only sitting over the arch of a casemate filled with two hundred thousand pounds of powder, but that the whole castle, which they had so rashly occupied, was undermined. "The rest you have seen," he said, "but of this you could not be aware. My riches are the sole cause of the war which has been made against me, and in one moment I can destroy them. Life is nothing to me, I might have ended it among the Greeks, but could I, a powerless old man, resolve to live on terms of equality among those whose absolute master I have been? Thus, whichever way I look, my career is ended. However, I am attached to those who still surround me, so hear my last resolve. Let a pardon, sealed by the sultan's hands, be given me, and I will submit. I will go to Constantinople, to Asia Minor, or wherever I am sent. The things I should see here would no longer be fitting for me to behold."

To this Kursheed's envoys made answer that without doubt these terms would be conceded. Ali then touched his breast and forehead, and, drawing forth his watch, presented it to the keeper of the wardrobe. "I mean what I say, my friend," he observed; "my word will be kept. If within an hour thy soldiers are not withdrawn from this castle which has been treacherously yielded to them, I will blow it up. Return to the Seraskier, warn him that if he allows one minute more to elapse than the time specified, his army, his garrison, I myself and my family, will all perish together: two hundred thousand pounds of powder can destroy all that surrounds us. Take this watch, I give it thee, and forget not that I am a man of my word." Then, dismissing the messengers, he saluted them graciously, observing that he did not expect an answer until the soldiers should have evacuated the castle.

The envoys had barely returned to the camp when Kursheed sent orders to abandon the fortress. As the reason far this step could not be concealed, everyone, exaggerating the danger, imagined deadly mines ready to be fired everywhere, and the whole army clamoured to break up the camp. Thus Ali and his fifty followers cast terror into the hearts of nearly thirty thousand men, crowded together on the slopes of Janina. Every sound, every whiff of smoke, ascending from near the castle, became a subject of alarm for the besiegers. And as the besieged had provisions for a long time, Kursheed saw little chance of successfully ending his enterprise; when Ali's demand for pardon occurred to him. Without stating his real plans, he proposed to his Council to unite in signing a petition to the Divan for Ali's pardon.

This deed, formally executed, and bearing more than sixty signatures, was then shown to Ali, who was greatly delighted. He was described in it as Vizier, as Aulic Councillor, and also as the most distinguished veteran among His Highness the Sultan's slaves. He sent rich presents to Kursheed and the principal officers, whom he hoped to corrupt, and breathed as though the storm had passed away. The following night, however, he heard the voice of Emineh, calling him several times, and concluded that his end drew nigh.

During the two next nights he again thought he heard Emineh's voice, and sleep forsook his pillow, his countenance altered, and his endurance appeared to be giving way. Leaning on a long Malacca cane, he repaired at early dawn to Emineh's tomb, on which he offered a sacrifice of two spotted lambs, sent him by Tahir Abbas, whom in return he consented to pardon, and the letters he received appeared to mitigate his trouble. Some days later, he saw the keeper of the wardrobe, who encouraged him, saying that before long there would be good news from Constantinople. Ali learned from him the disgrace of Pacho Bey, and of Ismail Pliaga, whom he detested equally, and this exercise of authority, which was made to appear as a beginning of satisfaction offered him, completely reassured him, and he made fresh presents to this officer, who had succeeded in inspiring him with confidence.

Whilst awaiting the arrival of the firman of pardon which Ali was reassured must arrive from Constantinople without fail, the keeper of the wardrobe advised him to seek an interview with Kursheed. It was clear that such a meeting could not take place in the undermined castle, and Ali was therefore invited to repair to the island in the lake. The magnificent pavilion, which he had constructed there in happier days, had been entirely refurnished, and it was proposed that the conference should take place in this kiosk.

Ali appeared to hesitate at this proposal, and the keeper of the wardrobe, wishing to anticipate his objections, added that the object of this arrangement was to prove to the army, already aware of it, that there was no longer any quarrel between himself and the commander-in-chief. He added that Kursheed would go to the conference attended only by members of his Divan, but that as it was natural an outlawed man should be on his guard, Ali might, if he liked, send to examine the place, might take with him such guards as he thought necessary, and might even arrange things on the same footing as in his citadel, even to his guardian with the lighted match, as the surest guarantee which could be given him.

The proposition was accepted, and when Ali, having crossed over with a score of soldiers, found himself more at large than he did in his casemate, he congratulated himself on having come. He had Basilissa brought over, also his diamonds; and several chests of money. Two days passed without his thinking of anything but procuring various necessaries, and he then began to inquire what caused the Seraskier to delay his visit. The latter excused himself on the plea of illness, and offered meanwhile to send anyone Ali might wish to see, to visit him: The pacha immediately mentioned several of his former followers, now employed in the Imperial army, and as no difficulty was made in allowing them to go, he profited by the permission to interview a large number of his old acquaintants, who united in reassuring him and in giving him great hopes of success.

Nevertheless, time passed on, and neither the Seraskier nor the firman appeared. Ali, at first uneasy, ended by rarely mentioning either the one or the other, and never was deceiver more completely deceived. His security was so great that he loudly congratulated himself on having come to the island. He had begun to form a net of intrigue to cause himself to be intercepted on the road when he should be sent to Constantinople, and he did not despair of soon finding numerous partisans in the Imperial army.

XI

For a whole week all seemed going well, when, on the morning of February 5th, Kursheed sent Hassan Pacha to convey his compliments to Ali, and announce that the sultan's firman, so long desired, had at length arrived. Their mutual wishes had been heard, but it was desirable, for the dignity of their sovereign, that Ali, in order to show his gratitude and submission, should order Selim to extinguish the fatal match and to leave the cave, and that the rest of the garrison should first display the Imperial standard and then evacuate the enclosure. Only on this condition could Kursheed deliver into Ali's hands the sultan's decree of clemency.

Ali was alarmed, and his eyes were at length opened. He replied hesitatingly, that on leaving the citadel he had charged Selim to obey only his own verbal order, that no written command, even though signed and sealed by himself, would produce any effect, and therefore he desired to repair himself to the castle, in order to fulfil what was required.

Thereupon a long argument ensued, in which Ali's sagacity, skill, and artifice struggled vainly against a decided line of action. New protestations were made to deceive him, oaths were even taken on the Koran that no evil designs, no mental reservations, were entertained. At length, yielding to the prayers of those who surrounded him, perhaps concluding that all his skill could no longer fight against Destiny, he finally gave way.

Drawing a secret token from his bosom, he handed it to Kursheed's envoy, saying, "Go, show this to Selim, and you will convert a dragon into a lamb." And in fact, at sight of the talisman, Selim prostrated himself, extinguished the match, and fell, stabbed to the heart. At the same time the garrison withdrew, the Imperial standard displayed its blazonry, and the lake castle was occupied by the troops of the Seraskier, who rent the air with their acclamations.

It was then noon. Ali, in the island, had lost all illusions. His pulse beat violently, but his countenance did not betray his mental trouble. It was noticed that he appeared at intervals to be lost in profound thought, that he yawned frequently, and continually drew his fingers through his beard. He drank coffee and iced water several times, incessantly looked at his watch, and, taking his field-glass, surveyed by turns the camp, the castles of Janina, the Pindus range, and the peaceful waters of the lake. Occasionally he glanced at his weapons, and then his eyes sparkled with the fire of youth and of courage. Stationed beside him, his guards prepared their cartridges, their eyes fixed on the landing-place.

The kiosk which he occupied was connected with a wooden structure raised upon pillars, like the open-air theatres constructed for a public festival, and the women occupied the most remote apartments. Everything seemed sad and silent. The vizier, according to custom, sat facing the doorway, so as to be the first to perceive any who might wish to enter. At five o'clock boats were seen approaching the island, and soon Hassan Pacha, Omar Brionis, Kursheed's sword-bearer, Mehemet, the keeper of the wardrobe, and several officers of the army, attended by a numerous suite, drew near with gloomy countenances.

Seeing them approach, Ali sprang up impetuously, his hand upon the pistols in his belt. "Stand! . . . what is it you bring me?" he cried to Hassan in a voice of thunder. "I bring the commands of His Highness the Sultan, – knowest thou not these august characters?" And Hassan exhibited the brilliantly gilded frontispiece which decorated the firman. "I know them and revere them." "Then bow before thy destiny; make thy ablutions; address thy prayer to Allah and to His Prophet; for thy, head is demanded. . . ." Ali did not allow him to finish. "My head," he cried with fury, "will not be surrendered like the head of a slave."

These rapidly pronounced words were instantly followed by a pistol-shot which wounded Hassan in the thigh. Swift as lightning, a second killed the keeper of the wardrobe, and the guards, firing at the same time, brought down several officers. Terrified, the Osmanlis forsook the pavilion. Ali, perceiving blood flowing from a wound in his chest, roared like a bull with rage. No one dared to face his wrath, but shots were fired at the kiosk from all sides, and four of his guards fell dead beside him. He no longer knew which way to turn, hearing the noise made by the assailants under the platform, who were firing through the boards on which he stood. A ball wounded him in the side, another from below lodged in his spine; he staggered, clung to a window, then fell on the sofa. "Hasten," he cried to one of his officers, "run, my friend, and strangle my poor Basilissa; let her not fall a prey to these infamous wretches."

The door opened, all resistance ceased, the guards hastened to escape by the windows. Kursheed's sword-bearer entered, followed by the executioners. "Let the justice of Allah be accomplished!" said a cadi. At these words the executioners seized Ali, who was still alive, by the beard, and dragged him out into the porch, where, placing his head on one of the steps, they separated it from the body with many blows of a jagged cutlass. Thus ended the career of the dreaded Ali Pacha.

His head still preserved so terrible and imposing an aspect that those present beheld it with a sort of stupor. Kursheed, to whom it was presented on a large dish of silver plate, rose to receive it, bowed three times before it, and respectfully kissed the beard, expressing aloud his wish that he himself might deserve a similar end. To such an extent did the admiration with which Ali's bravery inspired these barbarians efface the memory of his crimes. Kursheed ordered the head to be perfumed with the most costly essences, and despatched to Constantinople, and he allowed the Skipetars to render the last honours to their former master.

Never was seen greater mourning than that of the warlike Epirotes. During the whole night, the various Albanian tribes watched by turns around the corpse, improvising the most eloquent funeral songs in its honour. At daybreak, the body, washed and prepared according to the Mohammedan ritual, was deposited in a coffin draped with a splendid Indian Cashmere shawl, on which was placed a magnificent turban, adorned with the plumes Ali had worn in battle. The mane of his charger was cut off, and the animal covered with purple housings, while Ali's shield, his sword, his numerous weapons, and various insignia were borne on the saddles of several led horses. The cortege proceeded towards the castle, accompanied by hearty imprecations uttered by the soldiers against the "Son of a Slave," the epithet bestowed on their sultan by the Turks in seasons of popular excitement.

The Selaon-Aga, an officer appointed to render the proper salutes, acted as chief mourner, surrounded by weeping mourners, who made the ruins of

Janina echo with their lamentations. The guns were fired at long intervals. The portcullis was raised to admit the procession, and the whole garrison, drawn up to receive it, rendered a military salute. The body, covered with matting, was laid in a grave beside that of Amina. When the grave had been filled in, a priest approached to listen to the supposed conflict between the good and bad angels, who dispute the possession of the soul of the deceased. When he at length announced that Ali Tepelen Zadi would repose in peace amid celestial houris, the Skipetars, murmuring like the waves of the sea after a tempest, dispersed to their quarters.

Kursheed, profiting by the night spent by the Epirotes in mourning, caused Ali's head to be enclosed in a silver casket, and despatched it secretly to Constantinople. His sword-bearer Mehemet, who, having presided at the execution, was entrusted with the further duty of presenting it to the sultan, was escorted by three hundred Turkish soldiers. He was warned to be expeditious, and before dawn was well out of reach of the Arnaouts, from whom a surprise might have been feared.

The Seraskier then ordered the unfortunate Basilissa, whose life had been spared, to be brought before him. She threw herself at his feet, imploring him to spare, not her life, but her honour; and he consoled her, and assured her of the sultan's protection. She burst into tears when she beheld Ali's secretaries, treasurers, and steward loaded with irons. Only sixty thousand purses (about twenty-five million piastres) of Ali's treasure could be found, and already his officers had been tortured, in order to compel them to disclose where the rest might be concealed. Fearing a similar fate, Basilissa fell insensible into the arms of her attendants, and she was removed to the farm of Bouila, until the Supreme Porte should decide on her fate.

The couriers sent in all directions to announce the death of Ali, having preceded the sword-bearer Mehemet's triumphal procession, the latter, on arriving at Greveno, found the whole population of that town and the neighbouring hamlets assembled to meet him, eager to behold the head of the terrible Ali Pacha. Unable to comprehend how he could possibly have succumbed, they could hardly believe their eyes when the head was withdrawn from its casket and displayed before them. It remained exposed to view in the house of the Mussulman Veli Aga whilst the escort partook of refreshment and changed horses, and as the public curiosity continued to increase throughout the journey, a fixed charge was at length made for its gratification, and the head of the renowned vizier was degraded into becoming an article of traffic exhibited at every post-house, until it arrived at Constantinople.

The sight of this dreaded relic, exposed on the 23rd of February at the gate of the seraglio, and the birth of an heir-presumptive to the sword of Othman – which news was announced simultaneously with that of the death of Ali, by the firing of the guns of the seraglio – roused the enthusiasm of the military inhabitants of Constantinople to a state of frenzy, and triumphant shouts greeted the appearance of a document affixed to the head which narrated Ali's crimes and the circumstances of his death, ending with these words: "This is the Head of the above-named Ali Pacha, a Traitor to the Faith of Islam."

Having sent magnificent presents to Kursheed, and a hyperbolical despatch to his army, Mahmoud II turned his attention to Asia Minor, where Ali's sons would probably have been forgotten in their banishment, had it not been supposed that their riches were great. A sultan does not condescend to mince matters with his slaves, when he can despoil them with impunity; His Supreme Highness simply sent them his commands to die. Veli Pacha, a greater coward than a woman-slave born in the harem, heard his sentence kneeling. The wretch who had, in his palace at Arta, danced to the strains of a lively orchestra, while innocent victims were being tortured around him, received the due reward of his crimes. He vainly embraced the knees of his executioners, imploring at least the favour of dying in privacy; and he must have endured the full bitterness of death in seeing his sons strangled before his eyes, Mehemet the elder, remarkable for his beauty, and the gentle Selim whose merits might have procured the pardon of his family had not Fate ordained otherwise. After next beholding the execution of his brother, Salik Pacha, Ali's best loved son, whom a Georgian slave had borne to him in his old age, Veli, weeping, yielded his guilty head to the executioners.

His women were then seized, and the unhappy Zobeide, whose scandalous story had even reached Constantinople, sewn up in a leather sack, was flung into the Pursak – a river whose waters mingle with those of the Sagaris. Katherin, Veli's other wife, and his daughters by various mothers, were dragged to the bazaar and sold ignominiously to Turcoman shepherds, after which the executioners at once proceeded to make an inventory of the spoils of their victims.

But the inheritance of Mouktar Pacha was not quite such an easy prey. The kapidgi-bachi who dared to present him with the bowstring was instantly laid dead at his feet by a pistol-shot. "Wretch!" cried Mouktar, roaring like a bull escaped from the butcher, "dost thou think an Arnaout dies like an eunuch? I also am a Tepelenian! To arms, comrades! they would slay us!" As he spoke, he rushed, sword in hand, upon the Turks, and, driving them back, succeeded in barricading himself in his apartments.

Presently a troop of janissaries from Koutaieh, ordered to be in readiness, advanced, hauling up cannon, and a stubborn combat began. Mouktar's frail defences were soon in splinters. The venerable Metche-Bono, father of Elmas Bey, faithful to the end, was killed by a bullet; and Mouktar, having slain a host of enemies with his own hand and seen all his friends perish, himself riddled with wounds, set fire to the powder magazine, and died, leaving as inheritance for the sultan only a heap of smoking ruins. An enviable fate, if compared with that of his father and brothers, who died by the hand of the executioner.

The heads of Ali's children, sent to Constantinople and exposed at the gate of the seraglio, astonished the gaping multitude. The sultan himself, struck with the beauty of Mehemet and Selim, whose long eyelashes and closed eyelids gave them the appearance of beautiful youths sunk in peaceful slumber, experienced a feeling of emotion. "I had imagined them," he said stupidly, "to be quite as old as their father;" and he expressed sorrow for the fate to which he had condemned them.